W9-ATO-851

OCT 1978

RECEIVED
OHIO DOMINICAN
COLLEGE LIBRARY
COLUMBUS, OHIO

Goats, Sheep,
and How They Live

Goats, Sheep, and How They Live

Marie M. Jenkins

drawings by Matthew Kalmenoff

HOLIDAY HOUSE · New York

Text copyright © 1978 by Marie M. Jenkins
Illustrations copyright © 1978 by Matthew Kalmenoff
All rights reserved
Printed in the United States of America

J
599.735
J

Library of Congress Cataloging in Publication Data

Jenkins, Marie M.   1909-
  Goats, sheep, and how they live.

  Bibliography: p. 151
  Includes index.
  SUMMARY: Describes the physical characteristics,
habits, natural environment, and relationship to
humans of goats, sheep, and their relatives.
    1. Goats—Juvenile literature. 2. Sheep—
Juvenile literature. [1. Goats. 2. Sheep]
I. Kalmenoff, Matthew. II. Title.
QL737.U53J46   599'.7358   77-20149
ISBN 0-8234-0317-3

THIS BOOK IS DEDICATED TO
Sarah P. Faulconer

105747

Acknowledgment

I wish to thank the American Dairy Goat Association, the American Angora Goat Breeders Association, the American Sheep Producers Council, and the American Wool Council for providing me with pertinent booklets and information; and the World Wildlife organization for making available data sheets on the status of certain endangered species. Thanks are also due the New Mexico Department of Game and Fish for books and recent data on the exotic game animals in New Mexico; and Dr. Clair E. Terrill of the Agricultural Research Service, United States Department of Agriculture, for his kindness in sending me the latest information on chemical sheep shearing.

I am also grateful for the assistance of the librarians at James Madison University, Harrisonburg, Virginia, in obtaining numerous books and periodicals, and wish to acknowledge particularly the patience and willingness of Janis Pivarnik, Assistant Research Librarian, in securing certain information for me when I was unable to go to the library.

Contents

Georges Cuvier could tell a great deal about ancient mammals, fish, and other animals by a careful examination of fossils.

1

Hoofs and Horns

One night when Georges Cuvier, the great French scientist, was asleep, some of his students tried to play a trick on him. Dressed as the devil, one of them crept into Cuvier's bedroom. On his head was a grinning mask with horns. His feet were made to look like the cloven hoofs of goats or cattle. The other students crowded near the bedroom window to watch the fun.

The "devil" woke the scientist, announcing in a loud voice, "I am the devil and I have come to eat you."

Cuvier just smiled at the monster in a mask and said, "All animals with horns and hoofs have teeth that are fit only for biting and chewing plant food. Meat-eaters have claws on their feet and no horns on their heads. You are completely harmless."

The joke was on the students. They had forgotten what Cuvier had taught them about the law of relationships. Quickly they slipped away.

Many times Cuvier had shown his classes how well different parts of animals worked together. Beasts of prey use their sharp claws to clutch and hold an animal and rip open its flesh. Plant-eaters have no need for sharp teeth or claws. Their long legs make it easy for them to run from enemies, and the teeth are big and flat on top, with ridges that help grind coarse food. A creature that ate meat but had hoofs instead of claws would starve, for it would have no means of holding its prey or reaching the soft flesh.

As centuries pass, the bodies of animals undergo many changes. Always, if one part changes, another does also. Whatever happens, in each kind of animal the different parts still match, and can work together. This is the law of relationships.

Cuvier told his students it was possible to decide whether an animal was a plant-eater or preyed on other creatures just by examining a small part of it, such as a cheek tooth. He showed this to be true one day when he examined a jumble of fossil teeth and bones that were embedded in a lump of rock. Carefully he separated the pieces and studied them, then he said that teeth, skulls, and feet of two different kinds of animals were present.

Some of the embedded fossils were part of an ancient animal that was much like the tapirs of today. These are long-nosed creatures, related to horses, that live in tropical forests. The other bones and teeth were from a two-toed, deerlike creature that belonged to a great group known as even-toed hoofed mammals. Not long after this lesson, complete fossil skeletons of both kinds of animals were discovered. They showed that Cuvier had been exactly right.

It is easy to see that some animals are related, because different parts of their bodies are so much alike. Goats and sheep, for example, are more like each other than either one is like a camel, but all three resemble each other more than they do a lion. Sometimes animals that are said to be closely related really are quite different. A whale, for example, is more closely related to an elephant than to a shark because both whales and elephants nurse their young on milk. A feathered penguin is really more like a bluebird than a seal. As scientists studied the structure of more and more animals, Cuvier's law became a sort of magic key that helped to settle many questions.

Mammals with "Super-Control"

Animals most familiar to us are those with backbones. They are called vertebrates because each bone in the back is known as a vertebra. Fishes and frogs, snakes and crocodiles, and birds and mammals are all included. Over 30,000 kinds of vertebrates are living today.

Mammals differ from other vertebrates in a number of ways. They are called by this name because they have mammary, or milk-producing, glands, and newborn young are fed on milk for the first few weeks or months. During this time the mother cares for her baby and "educates" it. Young mammals that are kept separated from others of their own kind often are not able to learn to care for themselves properly.

Only mammals have true hair. Even whales usually have a few thick bristles on their chins. Except for a few that hibernate, or sleep during cold weather, the bodies of mammals remain at about the same temperature the year around. Excepting in a few species, hair forms an insulating layer over the body, and little air pockets help hold in body warmth. In hot weather, evaporation of sweat from sweat glands helps keep the body cool.

The brains of mammals are larger than the brains of any other kind of animal. One area, the part that has to do with memory and learning, has grown so much that it lies back over the rest of the brain, and is much folded. This arrangement makes room for thousands of extra cells. Because of

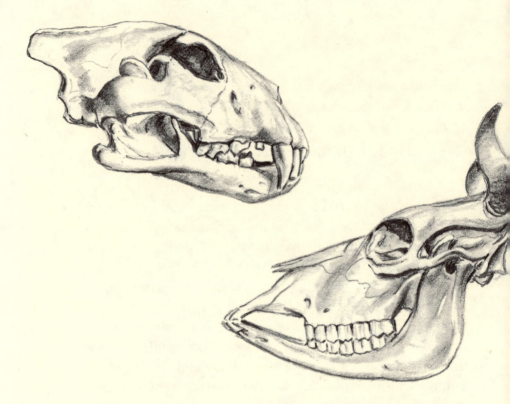

The skull of a carnivore, or meat-eater, can be easily identified by the large canine teeth, or fangs; a herbivore, or plant-eater, right, has no need for fangs but has substantial grinding teeth.

this, mammals have a "super-control" system. They are guided in their actions by the memory of things that have happened to them, and they can make choices as to what they will or will not do.

Teeth Tell Tales

Mammals have remarkable teeth. Each kind of mammal has teeth that are especially fitted for its way of life. Omnivorous animals such as human beings, that eat all kinds of food, have biting teeth in the front of the mouth. Next to these are more sharply pointed canines, or dog teeth. Usually there is one on each side, above and below. Cheek teeth, behind the canines, are known as premolars and molars, and are used for chewing.

Carnivores, or meat-eaters, such as wolves and tigers, have large, powerful canines that are used by some animals for stabbing prey. The premolars act as shears and can slice meat from the bone. Plant-eaters, or herbivores, sometimes have no canines at all, and the biting teeth may be only in the lower jaw, but the cheek teeth are large and rugged and can grind food well.

Creatures with Hoofs

Mammals are separated into about a dozen and a half groups that are called orders. Most of the large herbivores form a sort of supergroup. They are known as ungulates, which means "hoofed mammals."

Odd-toed ungulates, such as the horse and rhinoceros, bear most of the body weight on the third toe of each foot. In a horse the third toe is very large. The first and fifth toes have disappeared entirely, and all that is left of the second and fourth toes are two small splint bones, one on each side of the long foot bone above the hoof. The largest mammal that ever walked the earth belonged to this order. It was a huge rhinoceros, so tall that it would be able to look in the windows on the top floor of a three-story building.

Even-toed hoofed mammals bear the body weight on two toes, the third and fourth. The other toes are usually smaller in size or, in many cases, have disappeared altogether. Such creatures as pigs, hippopotamuses, camels, deer, giraffes, antelopes, and cattle are included in this order. Even-toed mammals are known as artiodactyls.

"Artio" means "even" and "dactyl" is "toe" or "finger."

Many of the hoofed animals, such as horses and antelopes, are swift runners. They developed long and slender but very strong legs, and ran on the tips of their toes. Planteaters cannot defend themselves well against the powerful beasts of prey, but fleet-footed runners can escape their enemies. The hardened hoofs, fitted for speed, are very important.

Odd "Toenails"

Hoofs, claws, and nails all develop in much the same way. A horse's hard, horny hoof is its "toenail." This has grown to be very thick and heavy, and it almost surrounds a broad bone inside. The underside of the hoof is horseshoe-shaped, with most of the space between the two sides being filled with tough horn sole.

Even-toed ungulates have two hoofs, one on each of the two main toe tips. Each hoof is much like that of a horse. Some of the even-toed hoofed animals, especially those that scramble about on cliffs, can spread the two hoofs and use them more or less as pincers when they cling for an instant to narrow or sharp rocks.

Ancestors with Hoofs

As far as we can tell from their fossil bones and teeth, the early ancestors of even-toed animals looked quite different from most of the ones living today. None was yet specialized for swift running or for eating coarse, gritty plant food. Some were squatty and piglike. Others were large and clumsy; a few were giants. One kind had peculiar

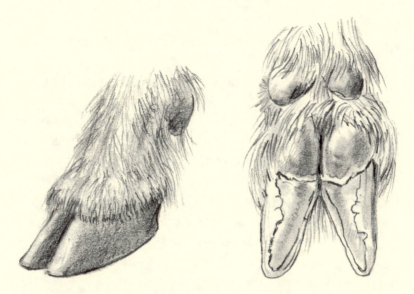

The hoof of an even-toed ungulate, seen from the side and from below

claws which it probably used in digging for roots.

As millions of years passed, many of the early hoofed mammals died out or became extinct. In a few families the animals changed very little over the centuries, but most of the others became quite specialized. Today the even-toed mammals are a quite important group, and are probably the best known of all orders because, with the exception of the horse, nearly all domesticated animals are included in it. Also, one tenth of all the different species of living mammals belong to this order.

The oldest and most primitive of living artiodactyls are the pigs and hippopotamuses and their relatives. These animals are much like their ancient ancestors and still have all four kinds of teeth. Piglike animals are omnivorous and will eat anything from grass to rats, but hippopotamuses rely on plant food. Small second and fifth toes are present in this group, but they are useful only when the ground is soft enough for the foot to sink in slightly.

Camels and their relatives make up the second group. These animals eat dry, scrubby plant food which is swallowed, then brought up later and chewed again before it is ready to be digested. The first, second, and fifth toes have completely disappeared. On the other two toes the pads are large and spread out, but are so grown together that they form just one big cushion for each foot. Camels can walk as well on mushy snow as on desert sand.

Animals in the third and last group are known as ruminants, or cud-chewers, They also swallow the food and bring it up again to be chewed, but the digestive system is much more complicated than that of camels. All kinds of deer and their relatives are ruminants, including the big, craggy moose of North America which is said to be able to fight off grizzly bears. Tall African giraffes with their small fur-covered horns belong here, as do the peculiar North American pronghorns which split off their old horns each year as new ones grow inside.

Hollow-Horned Cud-Chewers

All other ruminants are gathered into one enormous family of animals with hollow horns. Such creatures as cattle, buffaloes, and the elands and bushbucks of Africa are known as oxlike bovines. All the antelopes, including the dik-diks and slender, graceful gazelles, are hollow-horned ruminants. Goats and sheep and their strange relatives make up the caprine subfamily, the third group of ruminants with hollow horns. The caprine or goat-sheep subfamily is composed of the goat-sheep tribe together with several other tribes of near relatives.

In true ruminants the mouth, teeth, and stomach are

quite specialized. Cheek teeth, in both upper and lower jaws, are squared off and solid and have heavy grinding ridges. Instead of biting teeth in the upper jaw there is a horny pad over the gums. The tongue is long and muscular, and covered with little horny bumps. When the animal grazes it grabs and holds the grass with its sandpapery tongue and muscular lips, then crops the plant off by pressing its biting teeth against the horny pad.

Plant food is hard to digest because the walls of plant cells have in them a woody substance called cellulose that acts as a sort of skeleton. When plants are eaten, these cellulose walls have to be broken down before the food material in the cell can be set free for the animal to use. Chewing (or cooking) helps in this process. Chemicals called digestive enzymes break down and digest food in the stomach and small intestine, but animals have no enzymes that will act on cellulose.

A Stomach in Four Parts

Swallowed food goes down to the stomach through a tube called the esophagus. It has no enzymes and acts only as a passageway. In cud-chewers this food goes to the rumen, or pouch, the first of the four chambers of the stomach. It is very large and can hold a great deal. The animals fill the rumen by swallowing food as fast as they can crop it off. Then they can settle down to rest, or perhaps hide from their enemies, while small balls of food are brought up to be chewed quite thoroughly.

Great numbers of bacteria and protozoa live in the rumen. These minute creatures have special enzymes that can break down cellulose. Muscles in the rumen wall also help break up the food. Little by little, fragments of food mixed with a slimy mucus are passed to the second chamber.

When the animal chews its cud, small balls of partly digested food are passed back to the mouth, mixed with saliva, and ground by the strong cheek teeth into a pulpy mass. When this is swallowed, long ridges of muscle in the esophagus close to form a temporary tube that directs the food to the third chamber. In animals with short hair, these moving balls of food can be seen as bulges or knots on the neck that travel up or down.

Food is further digested in the third and fourth chambers and in the small intestine. Digested nutrients are absorbed by the blood, and the rest is passed off as waste. The organisms that help in this long process do not become part of the waste material. They are digested by the animal's enzymes and used as food that is rich in Vitamin B.

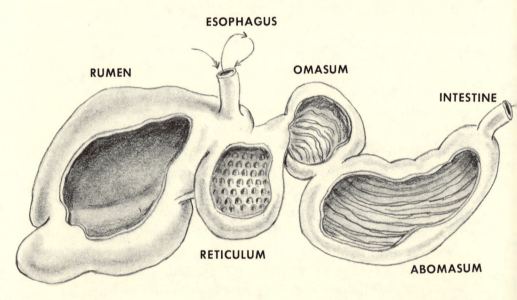

Ruminants, or cud-chewers, have a complicated digestive system.

Horns of All Kinds

Hoofed animals with hollow horns first appeared on earth around 25 million years ago. Since that time horns have developed into an amazing variety of shapes and sizes, from the short, sharp daggers of mountain goats to the great, curling horns of argali rams that may be even longer than the animal's body. Some horns stand upright on the skull. Others arch backward, curve forward, or become quite twisted. Often it is possible to tell the species of an animal just by examining these projections.

Females of many species have small horns, but only males produce the magnificent and often heavy head ornaments. True horns are never branched, and are not shed each year as antlers are. They are solid plugs of bone material covered with a horn sheath. It is the sheath that is hollow.

Horn bones first develop in the lower layers of skin on the forehead. Soon after birth, each horn bone becomes joined to the bone of the skull just below. Since bone is living tissue, it grows as the animal does. The nonliving horny sheath also "grows" at its base by the action of living cells; they exude the horny substance in much the same way that similar cells produce the nonliving hairs or fingernails that "grow."

Horns are used principally in fights with other members of the same species. As the animals develop into adulthood, they fight in order to find out which one is stronger. The winner can pester and "pick on" the loser, and the loser confesses defeat either by staying out of the victor's way as much as possible, or by such actions as licking and rubbing him. Young males, especially well-matched ones, seem to fight at any time just for the fun of it, but fights between big rams occur mainly during the mating season.

The Goat-Sheep Subfamily

So far as we know, the earliest ancestors of the caprines, or the goat-sheep tribe and their relatives, were big beasts now known as Tossunnoria. These animals roamed the hills and mountains of southeastern Asia around ten million years ago. Judging from fossil bones, tossunnorians were much like true goats, but they also greatly resembled certain goat-antelopes such as the chamois, a sure-footed mountain climber of Europe.

Two-toed descendants of these early ancestors spread slowly south and west during the next few million years. Other descendants of the tossunnorians spread northward, and a few even reached North America. These probably crossed over a great land bridge that more than once connected the regions we now know as Alaska and Siberia.

Ice Changes Everything

During the last three million years, great sheets of ice have crept down from the north three or four times. Each time they covered much of the land for hundreds to thousands of years. So much ocean water was frozen in these glaciers that the level of the whole ocean was lowered, and in many places shallow sea bottom was exposed and became part of the land.

What is now Bering Straits and the Bering Sea, between Alaska and Siberia, was uncovered in this way.

The sea bottom became a great land bridge, which we now call Beringia. It reached from Asia to North America and was as wide as Alaska itself. When these vast ice sheets spread southward, they crushed forests and buried everything in their paths. In front of them the chilled land became tundra. Not far below the surface the soil was frozen, and the only things that grew there were stunted trees and low bushes that could stand the cold.

Each time the glaciers advanced, Beringia was exposed, and became part of the tundra. Even when the glaciers reached as far south as what is now Illinois, much of western and central Alaska, as well as Beringia, remained free of ice sheets because the land was so low. Herds of sheep and other animals wandered freely over this huge, treeless plain for thousands of years.

During long periods of time between the growth of glaciers, the climate became a little warmer. The edges of the ice sheets gradually melted and shrank back toward the north, sometimes far into Canada. As the melted water ran into the sea, Beringia was flooded. It has now been beneath the sea around eight thousand years. When Asia and North America became separated, many animals were left in the new land. All of our native hollow-horned mammals came into North America in this way.

Mountain Living

Most members of the goat-sheep tribe and their relatives are well suited for mountain life. Many rarely seek new places to live unless supplies of food or water run so low they are forced to do so. This has led to groups of animals' being shut off from others of their kind by great valleys or forests, perhaps for thousands of years.

As a result, each group has developed in its own way, and animals in one region have often become quite different from those in another. Sometimes it is difficult to tell whether two groups, not more than two or three days' travel from each other, are so closely related that they are only varieties or subspecies, or whether each different group has really become a separate species. Even scientists who study the animals do not always agree on this.

Wild members of the caprine subfamily, like so many other forms of wildlife, are becoming ever more scarce, but domesticated sheep are found in every land and can be counted by the millions. A small number are pets, but many are important in business and trade; and a few are hated. Some of the most common animals in the world are caprines, and some of the rarest. All are fascinating.

2

Our Ancient Friend the Goat

Long before history began, early people roamed plains, mountains, and forests looking for food. They gathered fruits and seeds, dug up fleshy roots, and caught small water animals such as crabs and fish. Sometimes they could capture land animals that straggled behind the herds because they were old or lame.

Later, people learned to make and use crude tools and weapons, such as knives or spears chipped from stone. With these they could kill larger animals. Such creatures furnished them with a good deal of meat, and also with large skins that could be used for a covering against the weather.

Finally, primitive humans began to keep and herd small groups of animals. No one knows just when or how this happened, but probably it was through some accident. Perhaps a hunter captured a group of animals in a dead-end canyon and walled off the other end with brush and mud. Or he might have found young creatures without a mother and taken them home to raise.

Archaeologists, the scientists who dig up and study long-buried remains of the human race, think that domesticating animals probably occurred many times and in different regions. In many places, especially in southwestern Asia, bones that appear not to have belonged to wild animals have been found buried with bones and tools of early humans.

Ancient Bones and Horns

One such place is Ali Kosh, in Iran. It lies at the foot-hills of the Zagros Mountains, east of the Tigris River. This area is now part of a wide, bare plain that is blazing hot in summer, but grasses and other plants flourished there several thousand years ago, watered by winter rains. Archaeologists from both the United States and Iran have studied this site. They believe early people lived there for about 4000 years, beginning around 10,000 years ago.

When scientists are hunting for traces of ancient people, one thing they look for is a low mound that rises above the surrounding level and seems not to be a natural hill. Just such a low mound was found at Ali Kosh, and scientists began to dig there carefully. Anything they found was saved and marked, so they would know exactly what part of the site it came from and could study it later.

As the archaeologists dug more deeply they found that the mound was made of a series of layers, or levels, one on top of another. Each level contained what was left of an ancient settlement that had been built on the ruins of a still earlier one. In each layer was much rubbish such as broken weapons or tools, or charred or gnawed bones that had been licked and cleaned of the last bit of meat, then tossed away.

In "digs" like this the lowest layers are the oldest. These are usually quite deep below the surface. Objects found at different levels can be taken to a laboratory and tested so that it is possible to find out just how old each layer is.

At Ali Kosh a great number of bones and horns of both

goats and sheep were found, even in the lowest layers. These were so plentiful, compared to the number of bones they found of other animals, that it seems likely that the early people of this settlement had captive herds. Otherwise, if they had to get out and hunt, and take their chances on finding animals, there should not have been nearly so many bones of the same kind of creature.

Another reason for thinking the goats and sheep were domesticated is that very many of the goat bones were those of young males. At this age the males are rugged and fierce, and often are much harder to catch than are other members of the herd. Also, in one of the lower layers at Ali Kosh the hornless skull of a female sheep was found. This is another reason to think animals were domesticated at this time, for wild goats and sheep of both sexes have horns, but domestic female sheep usually do not.

Changes: A Mystery

Everywhere that wild goats and sheep have come under human care and begun to depend on us, changes have taken place. This would be expected, for the captured animals would have to be kept completely away from their wild brothers, or they might run off to join them. When groups of any kind of animal are kept separate and are allowed to breed only with each other, changes of some kind always show up.

Over the years, descendants of domesticated animals are likely to become smaller. This does not happen in the wild, because the smaller and weaker animals are more likely to be killed and eaten by beasts of prey and usually do not live long enough to pass on their weaknesses to any offspring. Only the strongest and best ones survive.

Herdsmen, however, might have preferred to keep smaller animals for breeding, for they probably could be managed more readily. This might be true especially if the females were to be milked. Other animals, and any young they might have, would probably be used for food. When ancient bones of goats and sheep are found and the bones of even the adults are small, it is a good sign that the remains are of domesticated creatures.

Changes in horns have also taken place in domesticated goats, and these are easily noticed. Ancient wild goats had long, backward-curved horns that were shaped like a scimitar. If one of these horns is cut crosswise, it can be seen that the horn core is somewhat four-sided. In domesticated goats this four-sidedness is gradually lost over the generations, and the core becomes more oval. Later, the inner side of the curve becomes flattened.

Why these changes take place is a mystery that no one has yet solved. Scientists think it is likely that goats were bred for something that the owner wanted, such as a greater amount of milk, and that the horn shape was linked to this characteristic in the animal's cells, and thus accidentally got changed also. No one knows whether or not this is the true answer.

Tracks in the Mud

One of the most interesting proofs that goats and sheep were domesticated long ago was found at Ganj-Dareh, a small mound in a mountain region some distance north of Ali Kosh. Settlers who lived here 9000 years ago built the walls of their houses of mud bricks that were laid flat on the ground to dry in the sun. Present-day villagers in this area build their houses in the same way.

When archaeologists dug here they were delighted to find bricks that had the marks of small, cloven hoofs on them. These were unmistakable hoofprints of goats or sheep. Wild animals would never have been bold enough to come into the settlement and wander around the huts while the people were working on them, and the mud was still wet. Domesticated goats and sheep still roam the narrow streets of many villages today.

Goats can pretty well take care of themselves by grazing on weeds and tough grasses, or browsing on bushes. They even climb low trees if the limbs are somewhat level, and munch on the twigs. Because of the large rumen with its swarms of little organisms, all this gritty food can be digested and used.

Although these animals can exist on poor food, both wild and tame goats seem to prefer leaves of all kinds, especially young, tender ones. They also like dead, dried leaves, even tobacco leaves that have been shredded and wrapped in cigarette paper. Stories about goats eating tin cans, however, are just tall tales. A half-starved animal may munch and even swallow a paper label from a tin can, or clothes hanging from a line, just to fill a nagging empty place in its stomach. Or it may nibble any sort of material out of curiosity or in play, but it never chooses such for food.

Goats are social animals and will stay together eating while one or more stands guard. If a hungry predator creeps close, the lookout sounds an alarm, and the animals run madly for any rocky crags or other hiding places nearby. A goat can scramble up nearly sheer cliff faces that are far too dangerous for other animals to try to follow.

Early herders must have found that goats were handy animals to have around. They furnished both meat and milk, and the skins could be used for many things from tents to food containers. Remains found in many digs show that goats were much more commonly kept by primitive peoples than were sheep, probably because they furnished so many needed materials, yet were easy to care for. In a number of early settlements studied, as high as 80 per cent of the bones found in rubbish piles have been those of goats.

Wild Goats

The bezoar, or true wild goat of southwestern Asia, is thought to be very much like the ancestor of today's domesticated goats. The odd name comes from the tightly matted balls of hair, or "bezoars," found in the stomachs of the animals. As the goats groom themselves, hair is licked off the body and swallowed, sometimes mixed with small pebbles or other bits of matter in the hair. This mass cannot be digested, and after a while the balls become as hard and smooth as rocks. Wild bezoars are often killed for their stomach stones, since superstitious people think that the stones have magic powers and can cure all sorts of sicknesses. This belief goes back for centuries. King Charles IX of France once had a bezoar that had cost him much money. It was supposed to cure him in case anyone succeeded in poisoning him.

The scientific name of the goat is *Capra aegagrus,* al-

A group of browsing goats in the wild makes sure of safety by setting a sentinel to watch for the approach of predators.

though *Capra hircus* was used for a long time. *Capra* is a form of the Latin word for goat, while *aegagrus* comes from the Greek word for the animal. The term *hircus* refers to the disagreeable goat smell. Female goats have no unpleasant odor, but males have scent glands under the base of the tail that secrete a strong "buck scent." In some animals this can be smelled for a long distance.

Wild goats are about as large as a small pony. The horns, which may be quite long, have sharply curved tips and narrow front edges with half a dozen or more knobs on them. Male goats have a thick beard hanging under the chin. Females are smaller and beardless, and have short, slender horns.

A White House Gift

Subspecies, or varieties known as geographical races, have developed in a number of regions. One of these is the Cretan wild goat or agrimi (*Capra aegagrus cretica*). It has a black beard and long, sweeping horns, and is smaller and daintier than the goats of Asia Minor. Many ancient forms of art such as cameos, seals, and bronze vases, some of them close to 5000 years old, show representations of this animal.

The agrimi escaped death during the Second World War by retreating to high cliffs that no one could climb. Not long after the war was over the agrimi was declared to be the national animal of Crete. Although laws are supposed to protect it, there is danger of its becoming extinct because it is often killed by poachers or by tourists who want the bezoars or horns as trophies.

When President Truman was in office, Kri-Kri, a young agrimi born in Crete's White Mountains, was sent to him as a token of friendship. The Cretans also wanted to show their appreciation of United States' aid to them. Since a goat is a bit lively, President Truman could not keep it in the White House, and it was sent to live at the National Zoo in Washington, D.C.

Feral Goats

So-called wild goats that are found in Mediterranean lands other than Asia Minor, or a few islands nearby, are not true wild goats, but are descendants of animals that were once domesticated. Remains of such goats that lived several thousand years ago have been found in a number of regions, including Egypt, southern Germany, and sites where Swiss lake dwellers once lived. Escaped domestic creatures that have returned to a wild life, and their descendants, are said to be feral animals.

The United States has many feral animals, ranging from mustangs and burros to swine, dogs, and goldfish. Feral goats have been reported in 27 states, from the Appalachians to the Pacific. Most of the goats group themselves in bands of up to two dozen and live on steep hills, canyon sides, and river bluffs.

The ability of a goat not only to stay alive but to do well on the poorest land is at once the best trait of the animal and its undoing. In the days of sailing ships, goats were often taken on long voyages to furnish milk and meat during the trip. Sometimes extra animals were dumped on ocean islands. With no enemies and much food they flourished and ate everything in sight. Many of the once beautiful islands are now eroded and bare.

In 1878 one male and two females were left in Hawaii,

and another pair was taken there 14 years later. Descendants of these few goats have grown to so many thousands that they have even stormed the National Parks. Since any plant serves as food for a goat, many of the loveliest blossoming plants, found nowhere else in the world, are almost wiped out.

Catalina Island, not far offshore from Los Angeles, is also overrun. A study made there by Bruce E. Coblentz, of Oregon State University, showed that the only solution to the goat problem was to get rid of the animals entirely. The fewer goats there are, the faster they reproduce, as long as there is plenty of food and there are no enemies to bother them. If a band of 100 is cut down to 20 animals, these will reproduce so fast that within four years there will be close to 90 goats in the herd.

Natural Balance

More than any other animal, the goat is blamed for destroying good land, whether it is forests, parks, gardens, or pastures. Yet it is humans who are really responsible. Feral goats, or their ancestors, either escaped from humans or were abandoned and left to shift for themselves. They did not come to a new land alone.

In their own homelands, where wild goats normally live, there are enemies which act as natural controls. Among native plants and animals everywhere there is a system of checks and balances which keeps the numbers of any one species to a level that does not harm others. This balance fails when we interfere, either by taking creatures to a new land where natural controls do not exist, or by encouraging one or more species of plant or animal that we want for our own use to reproduce in great numbers, out of all proportion with the others.

If it is under proper control, the goat is one of our best friends, but a goat cannot know it is destructive, or look into the future. We often can see the probable outcome of our actions but, perhaps thoughtlessly, or in greed for money or power, we fail to do what is necessary. Dust storms on once grassy prairies, rocky slopes where forests once stood, and lessened rainfall after marshes and swamps have been drained are all, in great part, due to humanity's neglect of natural laws.

Humans have been called the world's worst introduced pest. Yet it is humans, with their amazing brains and skillful hands, that can overcome these mistakes. We can plan, and carry out changes that will help provide for a better future. It is only by protecting living things, and their surroundings, that in the end we can save ourselves.

3
Gifts of the Goat

The peculiar qualities of goats, both good and bad, have been recognized for thousands of years, and many people have feared what they believed to be the ghostly powers of the animals. In folklore the goat became a wicked spirit or demon. If not the devil himself, it was at least a close relative.

Perhaps the queer eyes of the animals played a part in this. The pupils of a goat's eyes are not round, as ours are, but are oblong, with square corners. It is not hard for a fearful person to see evil in such an eye.

For centuries different parts of a goat's body have been thought to possess magic power. The liver was used to treat diseases of the eye, and a rajah in India was said to have been cured of blindness by this means. Celtic priests dropped melted goat's fat into the ear as a remedy for deafness. Early colonists applied goat grease, rubbed in well, to relieve the pains of rheumatism. In some places it was said that demons could be cast out of a person by having a goat breathe them into himself.

Goat expressions have slipped into our language. To "kid" someone is to make fun of him. A short, pointed beard similar to that of a goat is called a goatee. The term "scapegoat," meaning a person blamed for someone else's actions, stems from the practice of early Jewish tribes of symbolically loading a goat with the sins of the people, then driving it into the wilderness. The Judas goat, still used in some packinghouses, is a well trained animal that leads sheep to slaughter, then turns aside at the last minute and saves itself while the sheep rush blindly on.

Milk "Magic"

The most "magic" thing about a goat today is its milk, for this sometimes works wonders with newborn, ailing babies. About 6 per cent of bottle-fed babies become sick if fed cow's milk, because they are allergic to it, yet 99 out of 100 of these children can thrive on goat's milk, even from the time they are only a day or two old. Some older people, too, because they have become allergic to cow's milk, suffer from ulcers, eczema, migraine headaches, or other ills. Such persons can usually take goat's milk with ease.

Digestion of cow's milk takes close to two hours, but milk from goats can be digested in about 20 minutes. This is because goat's milk is naturally homogenized. The fat globules are very small, and the milk quickly forms a soft curd. Goat milk is very white, and its food value is much like that of human milk. If proper care is taken, and males are not allowed in the same building with the milk goats, there is no goat odor.

The domesticated goat is found all over the world. It is often called "the poor man's cow" because many families that can provide for a goat could not afford a cow. In poorer countries people have been keeping goats for thousands of years, but the practice is now spreading in the United States, too. Each year, as land becomes more scarce and prices rise, many are returning to rural areas where they can

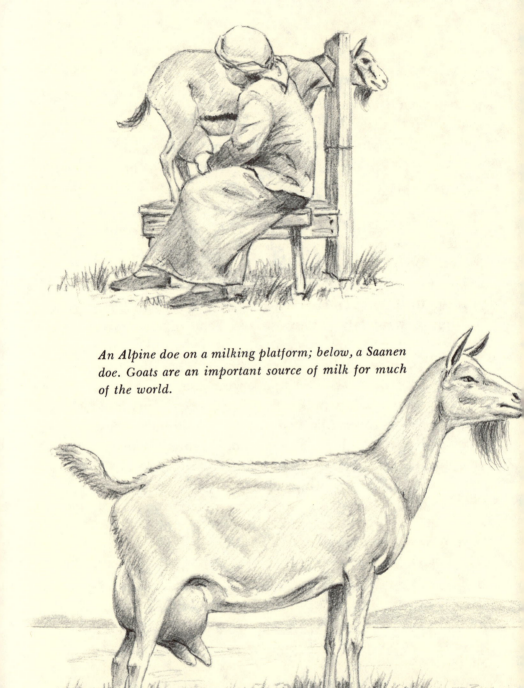

An Alpine doe on a milking platform; below, a Saanen doe. Goats are an important source of milk for much of the world.

live and grow much of their own food. The average family usually finds that a milk goat is a much better investment than a cow.

Many breeds have been developed. Though some may look different from others, all seem to be just variations of the bezoar, or wild goat. Meat, milk, leather, and hair are the main products of the goat that are sold, but milk is by far the most important. In fact, more people in the world use goat milk, and goat cheese and butter, than use the same substances from dairy cattle. India is the leading country in goat products.

In the United States there are five main breeds of milk goats. The males, or billy goats, are as large as a Shetland pony but the females are only about the size of sheep. The best milkers have long, angular bodies with thin thighs, and hip bones that jut outward slightly. A dairy goat will not give nearly as much milk if she has a thick body and short neck, or looks meaty or fat.

The Toggenburg and Saanen breeds came originally from the Swiss Alps, and the Alpine breed from the French Alps. All three breeds have erect ears. Toggenburgs are medium-sized, sturdy animals, with light to dark brown color and several distinct white markings. Saanens are slightly larger and are white to cream-colored all over. The Alpine is the largest of the three, and can have almost any variety of color or markings. The other two breeds, La Manchas and Nubians, also have coats of almost any color.

All five breeds are good milkers. The Nubian usually gives a little less than the other four, but her milk is rich in butterfat. A well-cared-for goat will produce a half-pailful of milk a day for eight to ten months of the year.

Two other main breeds of milk goats raised in this country are the Nubian, above, and the Toggenburg. Goat milk, which is digested easily and quickly by humans, is a great help to infants that are allergic to cow milk. Its food value is very similar.

Sometimes the animals are milked for two years before they are bred again.

Breeding Goats

The female, called a doe or nanny goat, is not fully grown until she is two years old, but she can be bred at the end of her first year. In the United States the breeding season runs from about September to January, or a little longer. During the mating season a doe comes in heat—is ready to mate—about every three weeks. At this time her internal organs can produce eggs. Each heat period last from a few hours to one or two days, and during this stage she will go after a mate. She usually rubs her neck or body against him at first, but soon will stand still so the male can mount her. If other females are near she will try to drive them away.

When the two animals mate, a thick fluid from the male, containing sperm cells, is discharged into the vagina of the female. This is a small passageway that leads to the uterus, or womb, where the young kid develops. Sperm cells swim through the uterus and on into a pair of tubes through which the eggs must pass in order to reach the womb. When an egg cell and a sperm cell meet and unite with each other, the egg is fertilized. It can then begin developing into a young animal.

Goats often have twin kids, and sometimes triplets or even quadruplets. From the time the egg is fertilized until the young are born takes, on an average, about five months. All the organs, such as heart, lungs, and brain develop during the first few weeks while the unborn kid is still quite small. It is not until the last two months, when the small creature is perfectly formed, that great growth in size takes place.

If the mother has been serving as a milk goat she should be "dried out" and not milked during this time. Like any other mother, even a human one, the doe needs to rest now and to have plenty of good food so that she can build herself up and also furnish proteins, minerals, and other needed substances to the rapidly growing infant.

If goats are not kept in a pasture their ordinary food is alfalfa or clover hay. Root vegetables such as turnips, carrots, or beets should be given animals that have no grass. Fresh, clean apple and potato peelings are also good, as are cabbage leaves and orange pulp, for goats like variety.

Goat mothers-to-be, however, as well as young kids and milk goats, need extra nourishment in the form of grain. This is commonly given as a mixture of corn, oats, bran, and linseed meal. The grain should not be ground too small, for goats do not like dusty food and sometimes will not eat it. During the last two months that she carries the kids, grain should form one-third or more of the mother's diet.

When it is time for birth the doe becomes restless. She may chew her cud rapidly, paw at her bedding, and bleat softly. At a normal birth the two small front feet of the kid appear first, with the nose of the new little animal lying on them.

As soon as the kid is born the mother licks and cleans it. She licks the head quite strongly, and this seems to stimulate the young one to stand up. Within a few minutes it opens its eyes, then struggles to its feet. At first it is wobbly and may fall sprawling, but it is soon able to jump and run, or butt its mother in its eagerness to nurse. If more than two kids are born at the same time they must take turns nursing, for the mother goat has only two teats.

Newly born goats are about the size of adult cats. They gain weight rapidly during the first six months, doubling their birth weight within 10 to 11 days. Males grow much faster than females, and become a good deal taller and heavier than female kids the same age. Wethers, or males that are treated so they cannot become fathers, grow to be even larger.

Males destined to be wethers are operated on when they are about a week or two old, and the organs that produce sperm cells are removed. These animals become very friendly and affectionate and make good pets. They have no disagreeable odor, and the meat is tender. Those who keep herds of milk goats usually make wethers of the male kids, then sell them or use them for meat when they are about six months old.

A kid has only a single stomach when it is first born. One or two weeks later, about the time the young animal is beginning to nibble on hay and other plants, the pouch and other chambers of the stomach start to develop. In a fully grown goat the rumen is about four times as large as the other three chambers together.

Usually goats are born with small buds on their heads that are ready to develop into horns. If the animals are to spend much of their lives with people, horns could be dangerous, and the kids should be dehorned. The buds should be removed during the first week after birth before they start to grow, so that no scar will be left.

Horns and No Horns

Sometimes goats are born naturally without horns. Many breeders have tried to obtain a breed of hornless goat by mating two goats without horns, but no one has been completely successful. Hornlessness seems to be linked closley in the sperm and egg cells to certain other characteristics that are not wanted. Many of these matings have an effect on the sex of the newborn kids. Usually more males than females are born, and some of the animals are sterile and can never produce any offspring.

In one recent study, 1051 kids were born to pairs of hornless parents. Of these, 599 were males but only 378 were females. All the others were of mixed sex, and neither male nor female organs developed properly in them. Animals of mixed sex are called pseudo-hermaphrodites, or false hermaphrodites. A true hermaphrodite has both kinds of sex organs, and it can act either as a father or a mother. True hermaphrodites sometimes occur among goats, but are very rare.

Silky Fabrics

Some breeds of goats have long, soft, silky hair that can be cut off and woven into fabrics. Kashmir, or cashmere, is obtained from the fleeces of small, hardy goats that are reared in the Himalayan region of northern India. Cashmere is used in making warm but lightweight clothes such as sweaters, shawls, and suits. These articles are sold all over the United States, but the animals are not raised here.

The Angora goat, which produces mohair, is grown in

The Angora goat is the source of mohair, which is particularly soft and lustrous.

our western states, as well as in South Africa, Turkey, Asia, and other parts of the world. It does best in a mild, dry climate. Two bucks and seven does, the first purebred Angoras to be brought to the United States, arrived in 1849. Now there are almost 50,000 registered animals, plus many thousands not registered.

Angoras have drooping ears, and the straw-colored horns of the buck spiral slightly outward and back. Fully grown bucks are quite large. Does are much smaller and have short horns that curve backward and downward. The long coat in both animals is a pure, shiny white.

Mohair is first cut off when the kid is about six months old, and it is shorn again every six months as long as the animal lives. The first two clips from young animals are packaged and sold separately, because the hair is softer and finer than in older animals, and brings a much better price. Bucks produce a coarser hair than does, but the fleece of wethers does not become coarse until the animals are about two years old.

Mohair is a specialty fiber that is often mixed in with other fibers to increase softness and luster. It dyes beautifully and colors remain bright. Wigs, rugs, knit goods, laces, imitation fur, suits, and other articles are manufactured from it.

Parasites and Disease

Owners who want to have a healthy herd must keep a careful watch over the animals for, like any other creature, goats and sheep are likely to become infected with various diseases. Some can be transferred to humans. The same bacteria that are responsible for Malta fever, or Bang's disease, in goats and cattle cause undulant fever in humans, and it can become quite serious. Few cases have been reported in recent years, but dairy animals should always be tested for it, since their milk and meat are the transmitters.

Worm infestations are among the most troublesome illnesses. One common parasite, the stomach fluke, in found in cud-chewers in most parts of the world. The adult fluke, a flattish, pink-colored creature about as long as a thumbnail is wide, clings to the walls of the rumen by means of suckers.

One goat may have hundreds of flukes in it, and each female produces thousands of eggs. These pass out of the goat's body with waste material and are washed by rains into streams or ponds where they hatch into small larvas.

The larvas enter the body of a certain kind of snail and live there while they change into another form, now with a tail. These new larvas leave the snail and cling to plants along the water's edge. There they take the form of young flukes.

If a goat eats these plants, the young flukes are set free when the plants are digested. They swarm to the lining of the intestine, where they creep about and do much damage. The goat becomes ill, and may die. Finally the young flukes crawl to the rumen and attach themselves to the lining of the wall. There they become adults and lay eggs, and the cycle is started all over again.

Roundworms are often found in the intestines. These parasites do not have to live a part of their lives in a snail or other creature. Their eggs hatch in the pasture and the young crawl up on stalks of grass. Goats become infected when they eat the plants. Roundworms can be gotten rid of with proper medicine, but if the goats stay in the same pasture they soon become infected again. Animals need to be moved to another pasture regularly to prevent reinfection. After a time the eggs die, and the pasture is again safe to use.

Sleepy Goats

Goats are not often used as experimental animals, but a few at Harvard Medical School are helping scientists learn about the mysteries of sleep. Dr. John R. Pappenheimer is trying to find out if the brain, during the time we are awake, produces some kind of chemical that causes us to go to sleep after a while. He has found that the shape of a goat's skull makes it a good animal to use for the experiments.

If such a sleep-causing chemical is made by the brain, Pappenheimer thinks that it ought to ooze out and collect in the cerebrospinal fluid. This is a watery liquid that surrounds and helps protect the spinal cord and various parts of the brain. The problem is to get some of the chemical out of one animal and put it into another one, without harming either one. Neither animal can be put to sleep with an anesthetic, because the experiment itself is concerned with sleep.

Pappenheimer solved this by operating on a goat and placing two guide tubes down in the brain, then letting the animal recover before the experiment was started. The tip of one tube was in a small cavity located in about the middle of the brain, where fluid collects. The other tube tip was in a second brain cavity near where the brain and spinal cord meet. Both tubes were made of Teflon, a plastic that is not harmful to tissues in any way.

After the goats recovered from the operation, a hypodermic needle, such as a doctor uses to give shots in the arm, could be put down inside a tube whenever it was necessary, and a little fluid drawn out. Between experiments the tubes were protected by metal caps that were fastened to the goat's horns. Several goats were fitted with tubes in this way.

In the first experiment, Pappenheimr did not let the goats get any sleep for 48 hours. Then he took a small amount of fluid from a sleepy goat and put it into the brain of a cat. Several cats were used, and every cat got very sleepy. Then he did the experiment over again, using the same goats and cats, paired together, but now the goats were allowed to sleep during the 48 hours whenever they wanted to. This time the cats that received the fluid did not become any sleepier than they usually were.

The same kind of experiment was later tried with rats

and with rabbits, and the same sort of thing happened. If the animals were given fluid from sleepy goats, they became sleepy. If the fluid came from wide-awake goats, the animals that received it stayed awake without any trouble. Such experiments as these may help doctors learn what causes sleeplessness in human beings, and how to treat it.

Butt Order

A few studies have been made of social life in goats. Like all other animals that live in flocks or herds, each animal has its own rank within the group. In goats this is sometimes called the "butt order" because the leader can butt all other goats below him in rank, but no animal may butt another that ranks higher than he does. This rule is broken only when a goat challenges a higher-ranked animal and tries to take his place.

A scientist at Bar Harbor, Maine, wondered what would happen if he put a group of goats under stress, or did something that would "get on their nerves." Would they forget about rank order, or still follow it? He decided to try making them wait several hours for their food for a period of a week or more, and see what would happen.

It did not take long for the goats to become hungry and irritable. Soon they were so cranky and quarrelsome that fights broke out everywhere. However, none of the hungry goats butted his superiors. Social rank order remained very important.

Trained Goats

Although sheep can be herded by a dog barking at their heels, goats cannot. They are quite likely, instead, to turn around and face the noisy nuisance, ready to fight. However, they readily follow a leader whom they trust, whether it is a goat, a dog, or a person. Some goatherders in Mexico regularly put a young puppy in the pen where nanny goats and kids are kept, and leave it there. The puppy grows up, perhaps thinking it is a goat, and almost automatically becomes the leader and guard of the herd.

Pet goats are often taught to pull wagons or carts but Anthony, an 11-year-old wether that lived on a Connecticut farm, made a business of this. He appeared regularly in stage performances of George Gershwin's opera *Porgy and Bess*, pulling the hefty hero. Anthony was a member of the Stage Actor's Guild and even boasted an understudy.

According to Robert Ripley in *Believe It or Not*, goats can also be trained to pull lawnmowers. A shop in London, England, in the 1800s advertised a lawnmower pulled by a billy goat. The owner could ride the animal as he mowed his lawn. At the Animal Behavior Enterprises in Hot Springs, Arkansas, dancing goats are one of the features, along with piano-playing pigs and a raccoon that plays basketball.

"People" Goats

One who spends much time with goats soon learns to understand their different sounds such as little bleats of friendliness, sharp cries of alarm, or grunts of anger, deilght, or hunger. A goat also understands much of what is said to it, and will soon learn its name and come when called. From the tone of voice it knows exactly whether it is being scolded, petted, or invited to eat, and will respond accordingly.

A goat that is used to people will push against a person,

even a stranger, wanting to have its cheeks stroked or ears scratched. Always curious, it may try to "read" a newspaper over its owner's shoulder or, given half a chance, jump into a porch swing with its owner and "help" with whatever he or she is doing. Quick to take advantage of any carelessness, a goat that finds a gate unlocked, or a pile of boards near a fence, is soon out and gone. But it is not likely to wander far if it has a good home.

In return for affection a goat is likely to respond with a harmless butt. This is a goat's way of greeting a friend. Goats butt and have mock fights for the fun of it in much the same way that dogs growl and tumble each other about in play. They need not be angry, but they are strong. If you are ever near a group of goats, just don't let one get behind you.

Goats in pastures have plenty of room to run and exercise, but pets all too often are cramped into small quarters. A pile of boxes, a seesaw, or a springboard in the middle of the yard will help take care of this. In short order, twists, twirls, and flying leaps will entertain the neighborhood.

Elizabeth Nicholds, who retired some years ago to a farm in New York State to raise goats, says the animals are bossy and lively, but become mean only if they feel they are unloved. They want attention and will bleat at the top of their lungs or play some trick in order to get it. Goats, she is convinced, are more like people than any other animal.

4

Ibexes and Other True Goats

When Tutankhamun, the boy-king of Egypt, died one January day over 33 centuries ago, priests and their helpers embalmed and treated his body for 70 days. After four days of special ceremonies he was then taken to his tomb. A golden face mask set with jewels covered the young king's head and shoulders, and the innermost of the three coffins in which he was laid was solid gold.

Tutankhamun's burial boat, made of alabaster and richly decorated, stood nearby. The prow of the boat was in the form of a large ibex head, with gems for eyes. It carried an alabaster burial vault with a canopy over it, and an alabaster maiden to guide it. Such model boats were often buried in Egyptian graves. They were believed to carry the soul to a sacred city of the dead where it would be reborn.

The tomb chamber was filled with burial furniture and other objects the reborn king would need in the afterlife. One of these was a dagger with a golden blade that he could use for his protection in the next world. The sheath over the blade was also made of gold, with ibexes and other animals carved on its sides. This dagger was among the tomb treasures of Tutankhamun that toured the United States in the late 1970s.

The ibex was not worshiped as a god in ancient Egypt, but it was an important animal, reserved for royalty. Together with certain other fleet-footed creatures, ibexes were kept in the royal gardens. Painted scenes in Tutankhamun's tomb suggest that, as a young boy, he hunted them just as his royal ancestors had done. Other ancient peoples also held the ibex in high regard. Small golden statues of the animal have been found buried with Persian kings, and ibex likenesses often form part of the design in old wall paintings and tapestries.

From the Ice Ages

The ibex *(Capra ibex)* is a caprid, or true goat. There are several varieties, or subspecies, but probably the best known one is the European or Alpine ibex (*Capra ibex ibex*). It has lived in the mountains of Europe, especially the Alps, since the Ice Ages.

Alpine ibexes have small beards and short, brownish-gray coats with darker underparts. They look much like a wild goat except for the large, bulky horns. These have broad front edges with heavy, crosswise ridges, and they flare upward and back from the forehead in a great half-circle. In some of the older males, horns are as long as the animal is tall.

Ibexes live higher on the mountains than trees can grow, although in the spring they may feed lower down when fresh, green plants begin to shoot up. From spring until fall the males live separately in herds of perhaps 40 to 50. During this time the females, together with kids and young males, live in small groups of a dozen or so. Depending on their size and strength, young bucks join the male herds when they are two to four years old.

Males often fight during the summer. Some of these battles are sham fights between equals, but other fights

settle the rank order of the animals, especially if one is young or a newcomer. Ibexes usually rise on their hind legs, then run toward each other and crash their heads and horns together. Sometimes they cross horns and push with the forehead. One ibex often circles around, trying to get on a rock or ledge so he will be higher than the other. Then he can bang harder at the next clash.

During late fall and early winter, when the breeding season starts, the large groups of males break up and the bigger bucks begin to look for females. Any fights that occur now are likely to be serious. Sometimes one animal can force another to go away just by rising on his hind legs or lowering his horns. The threat is enough.

Young ibexes are born in May or June, usually only one at a time. Within two weeks the youngsters show considerable skill at climbing and jumping over rocks by themselves. At six weeks young bucks may begin to fight. The goat mothers are likely to gather around and watch the battle closely, but they rarely interfere. When adult males fight, the females pay no attention.

In the Gran Paradiso

Over the centuries ibexes were hunted more and more for medicine and food, and the great herds began to disappear. By 1700 all were gone from the Swiss Alps and a little over one hundred years later only a few dozen ibexes were left in the world. These lived in the Alps of northern

The graceful and sure-footed ibex is thoroughly at home in the mountains. Note how the spreadable hoofs can clasp roughnesses of the rock.

Italy. In 1856 Victor Emmanuel, Italy's hunter-king, set up a royal preserve in a mountain area, now known as the Gran Paradiso, and sent game wardens there to protect it. Safe from danger, the ibex herds grew large again.

Before the turn of the century the Swiss set up a game park and tried to buy some purebred ibexes from Italy, but Italy refused to sell. Finally, in 1906, they smuggled in a few and started a herd. Later the Italians relaxed their rules and began to sell stock to Switzerland, and to France and Austria as well. Now, seven or eight thousand ibexes roam the Alps. All are descendants of the few that were saved in the Gran Paradiso.

From Desert to Inland Sea

The Nubian ibex (*Capra ibex nubiana*) is a smaller, dainty animal. It has slender, well-knobbed horns, a brown body with black markings, and a white band around each leg just above the hoof. Nubian ibexes live in rocky deserts on both sides of the Red Sea and are found mainly where high, jagged cliffs rise steeply.

West of the Red Sea, in a small area of Ethiopia, are a few Abyssinian, or Walia ibexes (*C. ibex walie*). These are much like the Nubian ibexes, but are larger. Walias are in great danger of becoming extinct, principally because so much of their habitat, or place where they live, has been taken over by humans and made unlivable for the animals. At the close of the 1960s fewer than 200 animals were known to be still alive. They are protected by law, but poaching and killing continues.

The tur, or Caucasian ibex, is a sheeplike goat found in mountainous regions between the Caspian and Black

Seas. These animals were long thought to be a single species (*Capra caucasica*) but most zoologists who have studied them now agree there are two subspecies. The west Caucasian tur is found mainly in the Soviet Union, but the east Caucasian tur lives in both the Soviet Union and Iran.

Although not unusually large, turs are splendid animals with rich brown fur and huge horns that arch outward

The Nubian ibex has a beautiful set of knobbed horns.

and upward, then swing downward and inward until the tips almost touch. Hunters make trips to the northernmost parts of Iran for the express purpose of killing one of the males and securing its head and horns for a wall trophy. Native Iranians kill the animals, too, but they leave the heads in the mountains and bring down only the useful parts, the hides and meat.

Great Horns and High Mountains

The largest and most magnificent of the ibex subspecies is the Siberian ibex (*Capra ibex sibirica*). Big males are both tall and heavy and their massive, ribbed horns are often quite a little longer than the animal is tall. The coat is brown, with darker markings that become faint in the fall. Siberian ibexes live high in the mountains of central Asia, close to the snow line, and their bodies are adapted to long, cold winters. They feed mainly on sedges and grass, both fresh and dry, but when these are covered by winter snow the ibexes eat any weeds or brush they can find. Only a little water is needed and during the winter ibexes can get all that is necessary by licking the snow.

Does carry their young close to six months, instead of five, before they are born in the spring, and the developing young are thus well protected inside the mother during the worst of the winter season. Just before birth the mother finds a safe spot, difficult to reach, on the sunnier southern slope of a mountain, and the kid is born here. When it is two days old a kid can run faster than a man if it is disturbed, but for the most part it remains hidden, lying in shrubby thickets or under rocks, for about two weeks before mother and kid join the herd again.

Ibexes in the United States

Some years ago the New Mexico game commissioners and the Department of Game and Fish became interested in trying the experiment of bringing over some of the large hoofed animals of Asia and Africa, and setting them free in certain wild areas. There were two reasons: they wanted to help save certain species that were endangered in their native land, and they hoped to provide new game animals for hunters in New Mexico. Animals selected would have to be suited to a dry climate, and the Game Commission and the department had to make sure the new inhabitants would not take over land or food that was needed for native wild animals or domestic stock.

Ibexes were among the first animals chosen. According to United States law, wild, hoofed ungulates brought into the country must be quarantined for a period of time, be certified free of disease, then spend the rest of their lives in an approved zoo. Only the offspring, born here, may be set free.

In 1966 three male and three female Siberian ibexes were placed in a somewhat dry region of southwestern New Mexico where there were rugged mountains on the north and grasslands on the south. Grasses, mesquite shrubs, and other semi-desert plants covered the hills. Native mule deer lived here, and the two kinds of animals often drank at the same water tank. They paid little attention to each other, although the deer at times seemed to eye the newcomers curiously.

During the first four years only one kid was born, and it died. The animals were then moved to another pasture

in the same general area, and are now becoming adapted to their new country. The herd has increased to 50 or more, and the state expects to grant a small number of hunting licenses within the next few years.

Europe's Other Ibex

A different species, the Spanish ibex (*Capra pyrenaica*), lives in the Pyrenees Mountains. These animals are quite small but the horns are long and have a peculiar little inward twist at the tip. The coat is light brown but the beard and chest are black, and a black streak runs down the back and along each side just above the white underparts.

Spanish ibexes are among the most endangered of the larger animals of Europe. Five hundred years ago they were common in both Spain and France, but three of the four races are now extinct, due mainly to overkill by hunters since the Middle Ages. Only the southeastern Spanish ibex is believed to be still alive, but the number of animals is probably less than two dozen. Total protection is needed.

Corkscrew Horns

Markhors (*Capra falconeri*) are among the largest and most spectacular of the true goats. Males are as tall and heavy as the Siberian ibexes, and the horns are as long, but are very different in appearance. Markhor horns spread outward from the base, and are flattened and twisted into huge corkscrews. Some twists are quite open, but others

The horns of the male markhor, above left, are much bigger than those of females, and truly dramatic.

form a tight spiral with three or four complete turns.

Male markhors have a long beard, and a long, shaggy fringe covers the throat and shoulders and hangs to the knees. A mane on the back is somewhat shorter. Females have thin beards but no manes or fringes. The general color of the animals is reddish-brown in summer and gray in winter. "Markhor" is a Persian word meaning "snake-killer," but whether or not markhors do kill snakes is not known.

These majestic animals live in Asian mountains from western Iran to northern India. Much of their time is spent either just above or in the timber regions. Groups are small and usually include but four or five animals, all of the same sex, until the breeding season begins in November. Then bands of both sexes come together and form larger herds of two dozen or more. Fights among males now become common. Like ibexes, markhors rise on their hind feet, then rush to meet each other with a powerful clash of heads and horns.

Once markhors were plentiful, but they have now been wiped out in some regions. Part of the loss is due to poaching and illegal hunting, but a great share of it is the result of humans' taking over the animals' habitat for their own use. In mountainous districts where markhors live, herders use most of the winter range for domestic goats. World Wildlife reports that markhors in some places have had nothing to eat but leathery oak leaves. They have been seen, perched high in the crowns of trees, trying to reach the only food available. The ground below was bare.

Land is both fragile and precious, but soil is easily blown or washed away unless roots or plant cover hold it in place. With topsoil gone, food plants cannot grow. There has always been such a vast amount of land that the human race has never been careful with it. If one section became barren through overuse, people simply picked up their belongings and moved on to a better place.

Conditions are now changed. The world population has recently doubled and will soon double again, but there is almost no good land that is not already in use. Even if we should sacrifice all the wild animals in the world so that we could have enough food we would not gain much, for within a generation we would have to face the same problem all over again. This time there would be a far greater population, but no animals left to sacrifice.

If all wildlife vanished, nature's balance would be completely destroyed, and we would face extinction, too.

5

Goat-Antelopes: Mountain Acrobats

Strange as it may seem, the "goat" of the ancient pseudo-science called astrology is not a goat at all, but a goat-antelope. These animals are closely related to true goats and are like them in many ways, but are more primitive and probably resemble the ancestor of both groups. They are as nimble as true antelopes and can climb and leap about on cliffs where it seems impossible that any creature could gain a foothold.

One of the earliest of these goatlike "cousins" of the true goat was a rather strange animal known as the cave goat (*Myotragus balearicus*). Fossils of this creature are common in some of the caves on the Balearic Islands off the eastern coast of Spain, but they have turned up nowhere else. The cave goat lived during the later part of the Ice Ages and was known to early humans. Artifacts, or objects made by human hands, such as broken bits of pottery, have been found buried with its bones and horns.

The cave goat was a rather small animal, only about half as tall as the goat of today. It had short legs and a pair of short, pointed horns. The most peculiar thing about the cave goat was its teeth. As is usual in the goat-sheep family, there were no biting teeth in the upper jaw, but the front pair of biting teeth in the lower jaw grew into huge, chisel-like teeth with open roots. This kind of tooth keeps growing throughout the animal's life.

Biting teeth in the upper jaws of rodents, such as rats

and beavers, grow in the same way today. They are used for gnawing tough, hard materials. This gnawing wears the teeth down, and they must continue to grow if they are to be useful.

We have no idea what the cave goat ate. Perhaps it fed on lichens and mosses or gnawed the thick bark of trees. Whatever the food, it must have been gritty, because the cheek teeth of cave goats were always well worn, too.

The slim-limbed chamois-antelope of Europe (*Procamptoceras brivatense*), another Ice Age animal that died out long ago, had quite unusual horns. These grew first backward and upward, in line with the eye, then curved forward. They were not long, and in the male they were thick and set so close together that from a little distance the living animal must have looked like that mythical creature the unicorn. No one knows what special use these forward-hooked horns might have had.

Remains of a few other Ice Age species, now extinct, have been found. One of these, Merla's goat (*Hesperoceras merlae*), was about the size of a modern goat. A giant goat of the Ice Ages (*Soergelia elisabethae*) was a stocky creature as big as a present-day cow. This giant was a true goat and one of the largest members of the entire goat-sheep family.

Princes of the Peaks

Four species of goat-antelopes are living today. The chamois (*Rupicapra rupicapra*) is the only one found in Europe. Its name means "rock goat." They live in high mountain ranges from Spain eastward through the Alps, and on to the Caucasus Mountains east of the Black Sea, but few are now found outside the Alps.

Chamois have the reputation of being the most sure-footed of all mountain creatures. One can balance on a rocky peak no larger than the bottom of a teacup, jump across a rift in the rocks six times the length of its body, leap straight up in the air to a ledge high above its head, or dash up the side of a steep cliff at break-neck speed.

Such acrobatic performances would not be possible without the chamois' remarkable feet. The inner sole horn of each foot, which is soft and rubbery, acts much like the tread of a snow tire. When the animal presses its weight down for an instant, this inner section can cling to ice or a rock. The lower edge of the hard, horny hoof forms a protruding rim around the inner horn sole. These rims, which do not wear away easily, act as cleats and catch the animal if it should start to slip.

Both toes on each foot are very movable, and can be spread apart in such a way that they can cling to both sides of a narrow, rocky bump jutting upward. The small second and fifth toes form a pair of false claws which hang downward behind the cloven hoof. When the heel of the foot is pressed down, especially when the chamois is running downhill on a steep slope, these false claws dig in tightly and help the animal keep its footing.

The chamois is almost as large as a white-tailed deer. It has a short, black tail, very large brown eyes, and upright ears. In summer the coat is reddish-brown with a creamy patch at the throat, but the winter coat is darker, and is long and thick. Neither sex has a beard.

Down the midline of the back is a streak of long, silky hairs that stand erect when the buck is excited. These form a favorite trophy called the "beard of the chamois." A hunter who captures one of these animals is, by tradition,

The chamois is considered the most sure-footed of all animals that live in the mountains.

entitled to gather the hairs in a silver holder and wear them in his hat. Tourists who buy this trophy at a shop and wear it, without proving their ability to stalk and capture a chamois on a steep mountainside, are looked down upon by hunters.

Both sexes have rather short, black horns that are set close together and grow straight upward from between the eyes. The tip of each horn turns back and downward, forming a sharp hook. Horns grow very little during the winter but when new, faster growth starts in the spring, the horn is pushed outward by hundreds of new cells at its base. This new growth takes the shape of a distinct ring around the horn. By counting the "age rings" one can get a good idea of the animal's age. Such bands of new growth are usually found in northern species of hollow-horned ungulates.

During most of the year each buck lives alone or with one or two young males, but the does and kids form small groups. Chamois are frisky animals and often frolic or play in the snow. Several naturalists have reported seeing them drop down on their bellies in the snow, with the hind legs tucked under and the forelegs stretched out in front. They slid down the snowy hillside, then ran up the slope and slid down again. Chamois are not easily disturbed, but if one becomes frightened it gives a ringing alarm call that sounds like a whistle, and all the animals disappear rapidly.

Stiff-Legged Rivals

About mid-October, when the rutting or breeding season begins, a great deal of secretion is produced in males by marking glands that lie just behind the bases of the horns. The animals rub these secretions on tree branches, grass, or other objects, especially if a rival male is nearby. The marks are a sign for other males to keep their distance and stay out of the way of the one that was there first.

Bucks join the females at this time, and large herds are formed. Mature males chase the young ones away. Then the old ones square off, ready to fight. No other male may come near a female that a buck is courting.

Chamois fights are real. The big male that is challenged arches his back and circles, stiff-legged, around his rival.

If the other one does not give in and leave, the two then push and tear at each other with their crook-tipped horns, trying to rip or jab wherever possible. Often the two break apart and one chases the other madly, but if the one in front gets a good chance he will suddenly turn and either attack or chase the other. Sometimes one of the animals is killed.

Early in the winter when the rut is over, the herd breaks up into small groups again. The young are born in late May or early June. Three or four weeks before this, the doe goes off by herself and stays alone until a week or two after the kid is born.

Sometimes twins arrive. A young chamois can stand almost immediately, and it begins following its mother after a few days. About ten days after birth it begins to nibble grass, but keeps nursing for another two months.

Balancing Artists

North America has no chamois, but one of its most fantastic animals is the only other living member of the rock goat tribe. The Rocky Mountain goat (*Oreamnos americanus*) is as sure-footed as its European relative, and lives even higher on bleak, snow-swept mountains. It is one of the few hollow-horned animals that crossed over the land bridge from Asia to America during the Ice Ages. The animals are found from Alaska through Canada to Washington State, and eastward into Idaho and Montana.

The scientific name means "mountain lamb" but mountain goats are far from lamblike. They are about as tall as the chamois but have stocky bodies, heavy shoulders, and short legs. Both sexes have beards and long, shaggy coats that are creamy white all year. In winter the thick fur

covering on the upper legs makes the animals look as if they had on baggy pants. Along the midline of the neck and shoulders a patch of longer stiff hairs forms a hump.

The undercoat of mountain goats is dense and woolly, and finer than cashmere. In late spring and early summer it is shed in large clumps that catch on rocks and bushes. Indians of the northwest coast of North America used to gather masses of this soft fleece and weave from it the famous Chilkat blankets that were noted for their lightness and warmth.

Black, dagger-like horns jut upward, then curve backward slightly near the tip. They are thick at the base and, like those of the chamois, have age rings. Behind each horn, at the base and half-encircling it, is a black, leathery marking gland. The eyes of mountain goats are dark brown, and the mouth, nose, and hoofs are black. Sometimes in winter it is only these moving dark spots that show an animal is walking over the snow fields.

Sure-Footed Ghosts

Rocky Mountain goats were probably the animals referred to by Captain James Cook when he visited Kodiak Island in 1778, and reported seeing polar bears on high cliffs. The animals live in such scraggy country, high on the peaks, that few ever get a close look at them. As a result, legends grew over the years. Many firmly believed, for example, that if a mountain goat fell from a high cliff it would

It was probably the white Rocky Mountain goats that Captain James Cook mistook for polar bears in the late 1700s. They are now rare.

land on its horns and bounce up again without hurting itself.

These animals break all rules in adapting to cold weather. They never hibernate, and never migrate to lower, warmer slopes in the winter. At times they may take shelter in a cave or under a rocky ledge, but soon they are back in the snow again. Sudden avalanches sometimes take the goats unaware and they are hurtled to their death in some deep ravine, buried under tons of snow.

Rocky Mountain goats rarely run. They walk when possible, and their movements are slow and deliberate, but if it becomes necessary they can jump across crevasses or leap to narrow ledges slightly above their heads. Some years ago a goat was seen attempting to jump to a narrow ridge that was a bit too high and far away from it. The animal landed with its forefeet only, and hung on the ledge for an instant, for there was not enough room for it to pull itself up. Suddenly the goat thrust itself backward with all four legs, turned a flipflop in the air, and came down safely in the same place it had started from.

Ruling Females

Both sexes usually stay together in small groups, although older males may live alone. In mountain goat society females stand higher in rank than males, and a buck that dares bother an uninterested female may get butted away. During the mating season the male approaches the female of his choice from the rear, bending in a half-crouched position. This is a typical sign of submission, and it shows that he recognizes she has higher rank. Once the female lets him know he is accepted, however, he gives her the usual ceremonial kick with his foreleg and continues with the business of courting her.

It is only during the rutting season in the fall that males can be easily distinguished from females. Bucks have the peculiar habit, before beginning courtship, of sitting on their haunches as dogs do, then using a foreleg to throw dirt all over the belly and thighs. These dirty spots on rumps and thighs of males show for a long distance.

Mountain goats rarely fight. Instead, they threaten each other. Two stand side by side, head to tail, with backs arched and legs stiff. Usually one soon gives in and leaves. If not, a fight starts. The bucks beat their horns sideways, each trying to stab the other. Sometimes one is seriously hurt or killed.

The females give birth in May or June. As the kids become larger they have to kneel to nurse their short-legged mothers. With stubby tails wagging wildly they look much like little white lambs. The young mountain goat spends many months with its mother, learning where to find food, how to escape enemies, and other things necessary for it to survive.

If the mother dies, perhaps by slipping on a ledge and plunging down to rocks far below, no other female will let the kid nurse. Billy goats may challenge or threaten it, and even the other kids are likely to attack if there is no one near to protect the orphan. A motherless kid cannot live long. It may become the prey of a roaming mountain lion or grizzly bear, or it may just become stranded on some high ridge and gradually grow weaker until it dies, alone.

The Smallest Goat-Antelope

Members of the goral tribe are often known as rock goats, but they differ from the chamois and mountain goat in several ways. These animals live below the tree line on mountains, often where the undergrowth is dense. There are no marking glands at the base of the horns, but some scent glands are present between the toes. These leave a marked trail as the animals wander from place to place. Females have four teats, as cattle do, instead of the usual two teats found in the goat-sheep family.

The goral (*Naemorhaedus goral*), a stocky little animal not as tall as a German shepherd dog, is the smallest of the goat-antelopes. It has a coarse, shaggy coat, gray to dark brown in color, with a light patch at the throat and a dark stripe down the back. Males have a short, dark mane on the neck. Horns, which are found on both sexes, are short and curve slightly backward.

Gorals are found from northern Burma and Kashmir up through the mountains of western China into eastern Siberia and Korea. Some live in steep, dry gorges where the main food is stubby grass and thornbushes. Others make their home in craggy valleys.

Nimble gorals are sometimes called the "Himalayan chamois" because they can find toe-holds on ledges not as wide as their feet. A movie film, taken of a goral galloping up a slope covered with loose rubble, showed the hoofs had already left the loose rocks before they began to slip under the animal's weight. Like their relatives, goral does and young animals of both sexes live together in small groups, but the older bucks remain alone except during the mating season.

Gorals usually feed early in the morning, then wander down to the stream to drink. Later they climb up again, usually to the highest ledge they can find. There they may stretch out, hind feet tucked under and nose on forelegs, and lie in the sun all day. Others may sit on their haunches as dogs do, perched on some high rock. Gorals often remain motionless for hours, and the coat color blends in so well with the countryside that they are often not seen, even when in plain sight. If one is disturbed it warns the others with a hissing sound, and all may disappear.

For over a hundred years rumors of red gorals have come from eastern Tibet and northern Burma. In Tibet some of the people were reported to wear red fur coats. Little attention was paid to the rumors, even when the Earl of Cranbrook shot a red goral in 1931 and presented it to the British Museum.

In 1960 a rug of red skins was sent to the museum for the animals to be identified. After studying the skins, scientists realized the first specimen was not a freak, and there was a red species of goral after all. This new species was named after the Earl of Cranbrook.

The Goat That Is Not a Goat

The "goat" or Capricorn of astrology is the serow (*Capricornis sumatraensis*), a goat-antelope and a member of the goral tribe. Serows are Oriental animals and have never been found in Europe, Africa, or the Americas. Once serows were found all through southeastern Asia, from

Serows too have been much reduced in numbers and now live high in Sumatran mountains where it is difficult to reach them.

northern India down to Sumatra. They lived in steep, well watered gorges and spent most of their time in the forest or in bamboo jungles. So much of the serows' range has been taken over by farmers, and so many of the animals have been shot by hunters, that only a few are now left. These have retreated high in the volcanic mountains of western Sumatra where it is almost impossible for either humans or animals to climb. Sumatran serows are often called maned serows to distinguish them from two smaller subspecies found in Japan and Korea.

Serows are about the size of Rocky Mountain goats. The coat is a grizzled black to rusty red in color, and on the neck is a heavy mane which may vary from black to white. The animals are clumsy but sure-footed. When not disturbed they move slowly, but at the first sign of danger they sprint away with an alarm call that is a cross between a snort and a screaming whistle. At times, natives hunt the animals with dogs. They want not only the flesh and skin but also other parts of the body that are believed to have great healing powers.

Courtship among serows is much like that among other goat-antelopes. The male licks the female's mouth or other parts of her body, gives her a loving kick with his foreleg, and rubs his horns against her. Mating soon follows.

The kids are usually born in late spring or summer, and the doe may walk around while birth is taking place. Newborn serows can scramble about and follow the mother on the rugged slopes before their fur is dry. A year later they are fully grown and are ready to produce young serows of their own.

"Abominable Snowmen" and Serows

Some of the regions where serows live have long been thought to be the haunt of the Yeti, or "Abominable Snowman." In some of the Himalayan temples are scalps, kept as relics, which are said to be those of Yeti. In 1957 the relic at Pangboche, reported to be 350 years old, was allowed out of the country in the care of a Sherpa, and brought to England for study.

Scientists at the British Museum examined the relic closely. Judging from its size and shape, the scalp looked as if it would fit over and cover a large head. The hair was coarse and bristly, and individual hairs were reddish in color, with dark bands. The skin seemed to be of ordinary thickness. No trace of sewing could be found inside.

It did not take long, however, for the scientists to discover the true nature of the specimen. The "scalp" was skin from the shoulder of a serow, molded to the shape of a head. The British Museum still has no real evidence that an Abominable Snowman exists in high Asian mountains.

6

Strange Relatives

In October 1959 a curious animal named Gracie arrived in New York City on her way to the Bronx Zoo. Captured as a calf in 1958, she had been the pet of Rawang tribesmen in northern Burma. Now, with the aid of governments and government agencies, and the payment of $1200, Gracie was on her way to a new life. She was the first takin ever to reach the western world.

Newspapers found it difficult to tell about this unusual creature. The *New York Times* described her as a brown-haired, "cowlike critter that looks like a fattish goat without a goat's horns." According to the *Daily News* of the same city she looked like a goat and moaned like a calf. The *Herald Tribune* said she seemed to be a cross between a moose and a goat but acted like an overweight antelope.

Gracie was unhappy when she started her trip. Monsoon rains, mixed-up airplane schedules, and too much red tape kept her in Rangoon, Burma, for two months. Having run free with the village cattle most of her life, Gracie did not like cramped quarters. She butted the railings off her stall at the airport, and nearly tore off one horn. Authorities demanded that she be put in the zoo until it was time for the flight to begin.

In Athenia, New Jersey, a 30-day quarantine awaited her. The wall of the stall there was well over twice as high as she was, but Gracie nearly managed to get over it anyway. Once safe in the zoo, however, with room to run, she became frolicsome and playful again. A favorite game was to gallop up to her keeper, whom she loved, and hit him a loving but somewhat painful blow with her heavy head.

Trouble with Names

By 1966 the zoo had decided Gracie needed a mate, and purchased a young male. He came from the Mishmi hills of Burma and was promptly named U Mishmi. The price

The takins have no close relatives alive today; they are primitive animals that seem to be "left over" from the Ice Ages.

this time was higher. U Mishmi cost $16,000, the highest price to date ever paid for a zoo animal. This newest takin was described in newspapers as a quadruple cross between a musk ox, a Shensi goat, an American bison, and an African antelope.

Scientists seem to have had almost as much trouble as reporters in deciding just what kind of animal the takin really is. Some think it resembles the chamois and should be placed with the goat-antelopes. Others put it in a tribe by itself. Still others believe it would be better to create a special group for the takin and musk ox, another odd creature that is related to the goat. Both these animals are stocky and short-legged, and look as if they were related to both goats and cattle. For this reason the two are often referred to as ox-goats.

Judging from their internal makeup, both takins and musk oxen must have had a goatlike ancestor. Neither has any close relatives living now, but the two resemble members of the goat-sheep family more than any other group. Both are primitive beasts that are more or less left-overs from the Ice Ages. They have been forced by changes in climate and land forms to live in forbidding, out-of-the-way places, and have survived for tens of thousands of years with little change.

The Golden Fleece

There is but one species of takin (*Budorcas taxicolor*), although three races are known. The scientific name means "ox-gazelle." A takin is about the size of a small cow but is heavy-bodied and clumsy-looking, with high shoulders and a shaggy coat. Both sexes have heavy horns. Of the three races, the Mishmi takin is most common. Its coat is yellowish to reddish-brown, but with a blackish tinge, and a dark stripe runs down the back.

Shensi takins, which live only in a province of China, are sometimes called golden takins. One zoologist described them as "shining metallic golden all over the head, neck, shoulders, and upper forelegs, with the hind parts passing into pale gold, then gray, and finally black." The beautiful color of this animal is thought by many to be responsible for the legend of the fabled golden fleece that Jason is said to have brought to Greece from Colchis, an ancient land beyond the Black Sea.

Takins spend the winter in small groups of six or eight, but form large herds in the summer. They live in bamboo forests or brushy thickets near the timberline, and make winding trails through the heavy growth which they follow regularly to salt licks. If one is alarmed it gives a warning cough and all silently disappear. A takin is heavy but, like a rhinoceros, it can run swiftly for a short distance, even over rough ground.

Mishmi takins are not yet in danger but the two races in China are considered by the Chinese to be rare animals, and both are protected by the government. A number of endangered species that zoologists are trying to save from extinction have reproduced in captivity, but no attempt has been made so far to capture and care for rare takins. Since they are herd animals, it is quite likely that takins will not reproduce in captivity unless a group is captured and the animals are allowed to live together with some freedom.

Gracie died in September 1975, without having had any offspring during her 16 years at the zoo. Another Mishmi female, named Daw Miri, arrived in January 1968, but she is on permanent loan at the Catskill Game Farm in New York State. Only U Mishmi, the male, now nearly 12 years old, remains at the Bronx Zoo.

Shaggy Beast of the Ice Ages

Over a million years ago ancestors of the musk ox lived on the vast icy plains of north central Asia. From there they wandered far, reaching lands we now know as France and England on the west, and spreading east over the land bridge into North America. Some then drifted toward the north, and finally made their homes on islands within the Arctic circle. Others ranged southward. Their remains have been found as far south as Iowa and Kentucky.

The scientific name of the musk ox (*Ovibos moschatus*) means "musky sheep-ox." The name was not very well chosen, for the animal is neither a sheep nor an ox, and it has no musk glands, although the males do have a strong smell during the rutting season. Musk oxen are not quite as tall as domestic cattle. They have stocky, heavy bodies, short necks and legs, humped shoulders, and stubby tails. The body is almost completely hidden by a shaggy coat of long, dark brown hair.

Both sexes have horns, but those of the male are larger. They curve downward close to the side of the head, then sharply upward again. The bases are enlarged and join above the eyes to form a plate. In males this plate is as thick as a human hand is wide, and is elastic and as hard as steel.

Outer guard hairs of the musk ox coat are coarse, and protect the animal from rain and snow. On the back these are about as long as a hand, but they reach arm length on the neck, chest, and hindquarters. The light-brown under-coat is so thick that neither wet nor cold can penetrate it. In the spring, when this is shed, the animals look motheaten, for the loose hair hangs in masses and sheets nearly to the ground. This woolly undercoat is far softer and warmer than the finest cashmere.

A musk ox is probably better adapted to cold than any other animal. Alwin Pedersen, an Arctic explorer, one day hung the fresh skin from a big male over a post and snuggled a thermometer deep in the hair. The air temperature was well below freezing. Ten minutes later Pedersen took the thermometer from the coat and looked at it again. It was now a couple of degrees *above* freezing. Although cold is no problem, musk oxen can suffer from heat, for they have sweat glands only on the hind feet.

A High Arctic Home

When the last Ice Age came to a close around 10,000 years ago, and the great glaciers finally began to melt and retreat toward the north, more than 200 species of animals vanished. We have found remains, thousands of years old, of mighty mammoths with great tusks, giant woolly rhinoceroses, and beavers the size of bears. In Europe the musk oxen disappeared also, but in North America they retreated to the far north and those that were left found a home in high Arctic lands.

Snowfall in the high Arctic never totals more per year than in some of the states on our western plains. The region is really a bitterly cold desert. Musk oxen spend the winter on slopes blown bare by the wind, and eat dwarf shrubs, sedges, and grass. Stunted willow branches are a favorite food. The animals avoid the deep snow that gathers in sheltered places, for with their heavy bodies and sharp, horny hoofs, they would sink, flounder helplessly, and starve.

Musk oxen live in herds of half a dozen or more during most of the year, but in late summer 40 or 50 may come together. The big bulls gather harems of cows, calves, and young males not yet fully grown. All young males which have become mature are run off.

If a newcomer with his eye on the harem comes near a female, the big bull slowly marches out to meet him. About 20 or 30 paces from each other the two halt, then suddenly charge and slam their heavy heads together with a furious crash that all but splits the thick horn plate. Then the animals separate, back up, size each other up for a minute, and charge again. This may go on for hours, until one is killed by the other's sharply pointed horns or staggers off, wounded. If he lives, next year he will try again.

Males are fully grown when they are about five years old, but females often begin bearing calves at three or four years of age. Young animals are born in the spring when temperatures are still often considerably below freezing. Sometimes the newborn calves are frozen before the thick, brown curly coat has a chance to dry. The female musk ox, like the takin, has four teats, but only one calf is born at a time.

A young musk ox begins to nibble grass or shrubs within a week or two, but nurses for several months. It stays with the mother a year and a half or more, until her next calf is born. By the end of the first year it will be as heavy as a husky football player, and a fully grown male will weigh four times that much.

A Circle for Defense

Musk oxen seem not to be afraid of anything. For all their bulk, the animals can run swiftly over rough country, their long hair flying, and can make almost a right-angle turn at full gallop. When danger threatens, however, they bunch into a tight circle with the big males facing outward, their heavy horns lowered, and the calves and females hidden inside. Though they scatter widely when feeding, the defense circle can be formed quickly.

Hungry wolves, ancient enemies of musk oxen, rarely succeed in breaking through the barrier and getting a calf. One at a time a male musk ox will suddenly burst forth from the circle, try to gore a wolf and toss him upward, then quickly slide back into his place again. When the pack leaves, usually one or more of the wolves is injured.

This instinct served the animals well for thousands of years against beasts of prey, but when men with rifles arrived, musk oxen had no defense. They never ran from

Male musk oxen can quickly form a tight and belligerent circle to protect the females and calves.

attack, and the tightly bunched group made a perfect target. Whole herds were slaughtered.

By the 1850s not a single musk ox was left in Alaska. Herds in Canada were so reduced that traders began taking the animals from far northern islands. By 1917 so few were left even on the islands that Canada finally declared the animals were to be completely protected, and no more were to be killed. Since then the herds have been slowly rebuilding.

In 1930 the United States Congress appropriated $40,-000 to purchase musk oxen from Greenland. Thirty-four calves and yearlings were brought to the University of Alaska and their habits and needs carefully studied. Six years later the 31 that remained were transferred to Nunivak Island off Alaska's western coast, where a national wildlife refuge had been prepared for them. Under protection the animals prospered. By 1968 the herd had grown to 750.

Although musk oxen lived in eastern Asia during the Ice Ages, the last one had disappeared from Siberia over 2000 years ago. No more lived in Asia until 1964. In that year the Canadian government agreed to send a herd to the Soviet Union, and the animals were set free on Wrangel Island off Siberia's northern coast. This island is in the Arctic Ocean, and is not far from Bering Straits where musk oxen ancestors long ago crossed the land bridge into what is now North America.

Peking Pets

Two more musk oxen were sent to Asia in February 1972, but this time they went to China. These two were among the gifts that President Nixon presented to the people of China on his historic visit. Milton and Mathilda, however, came down with a skin ailment shortly after their arrival, and could not be put on public view until they recovered.

Finally, in June of that year, the two unusual animals were ready to be displayed in the Peking Zoo. They were placed in the center area, in separate pens but side by side. Since temperatures reach as high in Peking during the hot summer as they do in New York City or Washington, D.C., each pen was provided with two shade platforms and two water tanks.

The animals often nuzzled each other through the fence, but they spent most of their time going from one water tank to the other. Newspapers reported that crowds around the musk ox pens matched those around the popular giant pandas in the National Zoo in the United States. These enormous "Teddy bears" were China's exchange gift to the people here.

Milton died in February 1975, almost three years to the

day after he arrived. Mathilda, at the last report, was doing well.

The Bearded Ones

For centuries the Eskimos have hunted the musk oxen with bow and arrow or lance. "Oomingmuk," the bearded one, could furnish them with three times as much meat as a caribou. In that cold land a good supply of food was worth the risk of facing the big animals, even if a hunter was sometimes gored by the sharp horns.

All of the animal was used. Skins were fashioned into sleeping robes, or parkas or pants. Horns were carved into ornamented spoons, knife handles, prongs for fishing spears, and parts of dog harnesses. Bones were made into scrapers and other small tools. Even the long outer guard hairs were woven into mosquito nets.

In 1954 John R. Teal, Jr., began a ten-year experiment with musk oxen. Since the animals were so valuable to the Eskimo, he wanted to see if they could be domesticated for steady use. With the permission of the Canadian government seven calves were captured and taken to the Institute of Northern Agricultural Research, in Vermont, where Teal was the director.

The seven young animals became tame within a week or two, and both Teal and his family were delighted with their antics. Curious and affectionate, they pranced up to be petted or scratched behind the ears, or to snuff noisily at pockets or packages. One day the whole herd followed the family into the farm pond and swam with them, splashing and cavorting as if they were a group of puppies.

Teal found that a musk ox will soon learn its name and come running when called. It also learns in a short time how to open gates unless they are securely fastened. The animals accept visitors as well as family, but have no use for dogs. This was shown when Teal was in the pen with the animals one day, and his dog came up to the fence. Immediately the musk oxen whirled to form a tight circle, heads outward and Teal in the middle, and glared at the dog. They had accepted Teal as one of themselves, but a dog apparently was too much like a wolf to be other than an enemy.

The soft, silky fleece of the musk ox, called "qiviut" by the Eskimos, is quite valuable. It can be pulled off the animals in sheets in the spring, or combed off. Musk oxen cannot be sheared as sheep are, for the coarse guard hairs become mixed with the silky undercoat and are difficult to separate. Also, shorn animals often catch pneumonia and die. One musk ox will give about five or six times as much fleece each year as a cashmere goat.

Teal proved with the experiment at Vermont that musk oxen could be domesticated and cared for without difficulty. The same feed that is used for other farm animals can be given to them, but their bodies require only about one-sixth as much, weight for weight. No barns are needed, and the animals are easily rounded up when it becomes necessary. The wool will not shrink even if it is boiled, and it takes any dye that has so far been tried on it. Garments made from qiviut are almost as soft and light as if woven from spiderwebs.

When the experiment was over the animals were taken to Alaska. In order to enlarge the herd several others were captured, with permission. By 1970 two cooperatives had been set up, one in Alaska and one in Quebec, both of them staffed by Eskimos.

Villagers do the knitting, under the supervision of members of the cooperative, and the cooperative then buys what is knitted. Retail prices range as high as those for garments made from cashmere, vicuña, sable, and mink. Several famous department stores have asked for sales rights. Teal's dream is coming true.

Those who have worked with the musk ox hope that it will turn out to be one of our valuable domestic animals. However, musk oxen are not likely ever to become as familiar to us as goats and sheep. They are true ice age creatures, and are not well suited to live and flourish in warmer regions where most people live.

Nevertheless, if we can save the musk ox from extinction and at the same time make a place for it in our world, as well as become better acquainted with its affectionate nature and intelligence, we will be fortunate. Not many of the earth's creatures that were once hunted by cave men have been faced with extinction because of modern people's carelessness, then brought back to serve a useful purpose. The musk ox is North America's living fossil and there will always be an air of mystery about this most unusual mammal.

7

Goat-Sheep Puzzlers

Most of the time we have little difficulty in telling whether a familiar farm animal is a sheep or a goat. Sheep are fat and woolly and hornless, and often act as a group rather than as individuals. Goats have beards, and are lean and hairy and horned. If given half a chance one may butt a visitor and send him sprawling. However, there are many other differences, not as easily seen, which are often more important.

True goats have no glands on the face, but sheep have a gland in front of each eye that secretes a thick fluid during the mating season. Sheep also have flank glands on their sides and scent glands between the toes of all four feet. As sheep walk, they leave a marked trail.

Goats have no flank glands, and if toe glands are present, which is rare, they are only on the forefeet. Male goats, however, have a gland under the broad tail that is not possessed by any sheep. This tail gland is responsible for the heavy, unpleasant odor, what has been called the "stink" of bucks, especially at mating time.

Horns of males are different in the two groups. Goat horns sweep upward, then curve toward the back like an Oriental sword, and some are twisted like a corkscrew. Most female goats have short horns. In rams, or male sheep, horns grow outward from the side of the head, then form the beginning of a large coil that looks much like a short spring. Wild sheep are like goats in that both have a hairy

The Himalayan tahr is well furred and "collared" against the cold winter air.

coat. The heavy, woolly undercoat found in domestic sheep has been produced only by generations of careful breeding.

Half-Goats

Some members of the goat-sheep tribe have about as many characteristics of one animal as the other, and do not truly belong to either group. One of these is the Himalayan tahr (*Hemitragus jemlahicus*). "Hemi" means "half," and "tragus" is a Greek word meaning "he-goat," so the name is a very fitting description of this half-goat, half-sheep creature.

Tahrs are rather stocky, copper-colored animals with narrow faces, large eyes, and small, pointed ears. No beard is present, but the males have a long, silky mane on the shoulders, neck, and chest that makes them look as if they were wearing fur collars. Stubby, curved horns, not quite as long as the distance from one's elbow to fingertips, have a sharp front edge and are set close together at the base. Bucks have glands under the tail, but their smell during the mating season is much less strong than that of male goats. Female tahrs, which are about three-fourths as large as males, have shorter horns and no mane.

Tahrs are found in the southeastern part of the Himalayan Mountains. Of all the goats and goat-antelopes, none lives in a place that is more out of the way or harder to reach. The animals stay just below the tree line, but in regions that are filled with crags and precipices. Groups of 30 to 40 females and young often come out to graze in clearings, but old males usually stay alone.

When tahrs feed, one or more sentinels are posted to keep watch, but these guards seem to look only downhill for danger. Hillmen, who use the flesh as medicine for fever and rheumatism, make good use of this odd habit. Staying out of sight, they creep and climb around the group, and approach from above. The men can often manage to get quite close before being noticed.

Male tahrs join the herds in winter during the rutting season, and often have fierce fights. Sometimes these are along the edges of sheer cliffs. Once in a while an angry buck loses his footing during the battle and plunges to his death on the rocks below.

Beginning in 1904, several pairs of tahrs were sent to

New Zealand. No large mammals are native there, and colonists who settled in the islands wanted to be able to hunt. The tahrs were set free near Mount Cook on South Island, and soon adapted perfectly to their new home. Even the rutting season changed, and mating took place in the New Zealand late fall and winter, which is late spring and summer in their northern home.

Tahrs do not live as high on mountains in New Zealand as in their homeland, for there is much more snow. In the new land they had plenty of food and no enemies (except humans), and grew to be large and heavy. By the mid-thirties they were becoming a problem and the government began encouraging control shooting against them. Hunting parties now go regularly from other countries to New Zealand to hunt tahrs.

Rare Tahrs

Nilgiri and Arabian tahrs, although different from Himalayan tahrs in several ways, are usually considered to be only subspecies instead of truly separate species. Nilgiri tahrs live in the mountains of southeastern India. They are larger than their northern relatives, and have short, rough coats and short manes. The Arabian tahr is smaller and more slender than either of the others. They are found only in a few hilly and mountainous areas in Oman, and in the southeastern end of the Arabian peninsula.

Both the Nilgiri and Arabian tahrs need protection. Their numbers have shrunk greatly due to excessive hunting. In India so much of the land is being taken over for agricultural use that the animals no longer have a safe place to live. Tahrs are protected by law, and some are in sanctuaries, but poaching is common and little is done about it.

False Sheep

The bharal (*Pseudois nayaur*) is another puzzling member of the goat-sheep tribe. The scientific name means "false sheep," and the animal is just that, for it is far more goat than sheep. Many have suggested that the common name, blue sheep, be changed to "blue goat," but it is difficult to get rid of a name that has long been in use. The Hindi name, bharal, is coming more and more into use, even in sports magazines.

Bharals are small but have stocky bodies. The coat color is a slaty blue-gray but the underparts are white and a line of dark gray separates the two colors.

Bharal males have peculiar V-shaped horns that first spread out, then arch toward the back, much like those of the tur. They are nearly as long as a man's arm and the surface is ringed with many narrow bulges. Horns of females are only about one-fourth as long as those of males.

Bharals live high in the mountains, both in gorges and on plateaus and open slopes. They avoid brush land unless, during winter, food becomes too scarce. Sentinels are often posted while the group feeds. If danger threatens, there is usually no brush behind which the animals can hide and they are likely to freeze, motionless, in place. Often the blue-gray of their coats lets them remain unseen against the slate-colored rocks. If bharals do have to run they can sprint up cliffs in a hurry.

Most of the year the animals live in large herds made

up of both males and females. In September the herds break up for a month or two into small groups of one male and several females. Fights occur often, and bharal males fight much as goats do, with each trying to bash the other with his horns.

Female bharals sometimes fight, too, behaving more like female goats than shy, passive ewes. One or two young are born in the spring. Like most members of the goat-sheep tribe, bharal females have two teats.

African Sheep-Goats

Aoudads (*Ammotragus lervia*), often called maned or Barbary sheep, are powerfully built animals somewhat taller than the bharal. Males weigh as much as a tall, strong man, but females are less than half as heavy. Stout, ridged horns in the male are longer than a man's arm. No beard is present, but aoudads have a stiff, hairy coat with a short mane on the back of the neck and a longer, soft mane that runs from the throat down the chest. In old males this may hang from the chin almost to the ground. A long fringe of hair encircles the forelegs and makes the animals look as if they were wearing pantaloons. Except for a few touches of white, the entire animal is a tawny brown. This color blends with the desert regions where aoudads live and, like the bharal, the animals can "hide" by remaining motionless.

Aoudads are the only members of the goat-sheep family that are native to Africa. Most of their lives are spent in desert mountains and they walk easily along almost perpendicular cliff faces. Males are no exception. They simply hold their heads sidewise to balance their great horns and move steadily along.

In summer aoudads eat grass, stunted bushes, and other scrubby plants, but in winter they settle for lichens and dry grass. Like goats, they can do well on poor food. Although aoudads like water, and delight in wallowing in a muddy pool if one can be found, they can get along with little or no drinking water. Enough moisture can be obtained from the dew that condenses on rocks and other objects during cold desert nights, and from green plants they eat.

The scientific name of the aoudad means "sheep-goat." Like the bharal it is an in-between creature, but it is far more goat than sheep. Warren Page, writing about aoudads in *Field and Stream,* quoted a hunter as saying, "No self-respecting sheep could live in this tangle of gullies and rotten-rock cliffs without breaking its neck. These critters have to be goats."

Aoudads are as good at jumping as they are at climbing. At the Frankfurt Zoo, in Germany, when some of the animals were to be taken elsewhere, several keepers carrying nets went into their pen to capture them. Immediately every animal jumped over the fence, which was higher than a man's head. The flustered keepers rushed outside to prevent the animals' escaping and, one after another, all the aoudads jumped right back into the pen again.

Rams or bucks live alone most of the year, but join the small groups of females and young during the rutting season in November. When males fight, two face one another for an instant, 20 or 30 paces apart, then start toward each other. Almost immediately they break into a run, lower their horns, and crash head-on. If something happens to throw one off balance, the other does not attack. Sometimes, instead of banging heads, the two stand side by side, head

Aoudads have a soft mane that runs down the throat and chest and encircles their forelegs.

to tail, and one reaches a horn over the other's back, trying to force his rival down. Aoudads may also lock horns and "Indian-wrestle."

The young are born in early spring. Twins are not unusual, and triplets sometimes appear. Young animals nurse for six months but, like most other goats and sheep, begin to nibble grass when they are but a week or two old.

Four-Footed Refugees

In January 1950, a number of years before ibexes were set free in New Mexico, the State Game Commission obtained four pairs of aoudads from the McKnight ranch in New Mexico and released them in one of the Canadian River canyons in the northeastern part of the state. Later that year a small herd of the animals, secured from the Hearst ranch in California, was placed in another section of the canyon. Eleven lambs were in this group.

The long Canadian Canyon is a rugged, mountainous region with deep gorges and many winding secondary canyons. Rainfall is usually slight, but flash floods from a cloudburst sometimes roar headlong down the ravines. In a short time the air and sky may again be filled with swirling dust. Aoudads are tough and hardy, however, and they adapted well to the environment.

Four years later the number of animals had reached 400 or more, and in 1957 hunts were conducted. Before long the herd had been brought down to the danger point, and hunting was stopped for a time. The population in 1977 was over 3000.

Aoudads have done well in zoos in all parts of the world and have the reputation of being the hardiest of all ungulates and the easiest to raise. If they are protected from harsh weather they seem to be able to adjust to almost any climate. Dr. Theodore H. Reed, Director of the National Zoo at Washington, D.C., has said that "it seems that all we did was put a male and female in a pen and stand back and watch them [the herd] grow."

Perhaps this is as well, for these striking animals with

their hairy pants stand little chance in their African home-land. For the most part, native Africans stalk and take the animals when they please, with no regard for their shrinking numbers. The animals are not yet on the endangered list, but no laws protect them and it is only a matter of time until all will be wiped out.

8

Rams with Curly Horns

Fossils of true sheep are very rare, and even these few are widely scattered, ranging from England to China. Bones of one species, discovered in France, are not greatly different from bones of sheep today. These have been given the name *Ovis antiqua*, the "antique" sheep.

There is much evidence that the earliest sheep, as well as goats, had their beginnings in southeastern Asia, and the largest and most magnificent of all wild sheep still lives in the mountains of central Asia today. We know this animal as the "argali," a Mongolian word for "wild ram." The scientific name given to argalis (*Ovis ammon*) refers to Egyptian gods that were worshipped nearly 2000 years B.C.

Amon or Amun, the Egyptian ramlike god, was given the names "king of the gods" and "lord of the thrones of the two kingdoms," which means the upper and lower Nile. He was also believed to be the creator, the god of the sun, and father of all the other gods. Greeks called him "Amon" and considered him to be the same as their Zeus.

Pictures and statues usually show Amun in human form, but with the head and horns of a ram, for this was one of his sacred animals. When one of the young Egyptian princes, Tutankhaten, became king over 33 centuries ago, he changed the ending of his name as part of an effort to bring back the worship of the ram god, Amun. Today we know this young king as Tutankhamun.

Argalis in Asia

Giant Siberian argalis (*Ovis ammon ammon*), largest of all living wild sheep, are half again as large as Shetland ponies. They are found in the Altai Mountains that run eastward from Siberia into northwestern China, near the border of Mongolia. Most of the land is rolling hills covered by rich grassland, with no bushes or trees. Here and there a steep, rocky gully drains away melting snow left by winter blizzards.

The coat of argalis is a grizzled gray-brown, shading to a darker brown on the neck and upper body. Belly and rump patch are white. Creamy or white rump patches on the rear are characteristic of all sheep. They vary in size from one species to another, and in some also vary with age.

Stories Horns Tell

The horns of argalis are monstrous. As in all true sheep they rise from the forehead, but spread apart at once to form a V. They sweep outward and back, then down and forward past the jaw, and up again. In an old ram looked at from the side, this curve looks like the first turn of a spiral. Often a part of the horn curve blocks off the sight of the eye beside it for some distance. Soon after young rams reach their prime, when they are about four to five years old, their horns are long enough to form a three-quarter curl.

The curve of the horn never makes a complete circle, no matter how old the animal becomes or how long the horns grow. Instead, it forms the first part of the coil of what is known as a golden or equiangular spiral. This kind of

The horns of male argalis are spectacular in appearance and unusually heavy.

spiral grows rapidly larger with every turn. The same peculiar type of twist is found in many things in nature, from the arrangement of pine cone scales and sunflower seeds to many snail shells and hair whorls on the human head, and from the hearing apparatus in the middle ear to the tail of a comet. The great value of this kind of curve is that it allows growth to take place without having to change form in any way.

To one who knows horns, each pair is as individual as a set of human fingerprints, but there are group or species differences, too. Argali horns pinch in close to the cheeks, then flare widely outward. They are flat-sided and large at the base, and have very heavy ridges and grooves.

Horns of Siberian argalis weigh more and are bigger around at the base than those of any other sheep. Each horn weighs about as much as a heavy standard typewriter. Both horns, together with the skull, make up about 13 per cent of the animal's weight. Some of the biggest horns ever found were discovered lying on a mountainside, along with the skeleton of the animal. Probably the ram had been trapped in deep snow and died of starvation.

Horns of old rams are usually "broomed" or worn off at the tips. Judging from the size of the broken end, a piece as long as one's fingers or hand may be missing. Most of the breakage and splintering is the result of fighting, although accidents may cause some damage.

Courtship on High Plains

Argalis and other Asiatic sheep seem to prefer to live in more or less protected valleys or on wide tablelands high in the mountains, and to leave steep cliffs and precipices to wild goats. They like to run and jump but are not good at leaping or climbing. Argalis are likely to refuse even to try to jump over a shoulder-high fence. In keeping with their running ability, Asiatic sheep are long-legged and light-boned, and are more lean than stocky.

Argalis live in large herds on the open hills but old rams, especially in summer, wander off alone and live higher on the mountains. If one senses danger he gives a snort of alarm and strikes the ground with his forefeet as a warning signal, and the entire herd races off in a split second. A short distance away, however, the sheep usually stop and calmly begin grazing again.

These animals can see well for long distances, and have a very good sense of smell, but hearing is much less important to them. In front of the eyes are eye glands which form a level slit, beginning near the inner corner of the eye. Each has a whorl of long hair just in front of it. A waxy secretion that soon evaporates oozes from the glands, especially during the mating season.

Courtship behavior is much the same in all sheep, but fighting is not. Argali males paw the ground spiritedly, then rise on their hind legs to charge. Each ram hits his rival with the narrow edge of one horn, putting all his force in one spot much as a karate fighter does when he strikes with the edge of his hand. Instantly the quicker ram stiffens and turns his head upward, thus hitting the other horn of his rival, then he kicks up his rear legs, driving the blow home.

Imprinting After Birth

Ewes give birth out in the open. Not long before time for the lamb to arrive, the mother becomes restless, and soon paws a bed in some quiet place. The young one is dropped, wet, onto the cold ground, and would die if it were not licked dry and allowed to feed almost immediately.

This licking also helps "imprint" the ewe on the young one so that the lamb accepts this ewe, and no other, as its mother. The ewe also learns that this particular lamb is hers, and will refuse to let any other lamb nurse. If something happens to the mother just after birth, the lamb will follow any passing object, usually the fastest, and become imprinted with it.

This firm bond is not set up if mother and newborn are separated after birth for as little as half an hour. When the two do not learn to recognize each other the lamb soon becomes lost and neglected. It will not grow normally, and soon dies.

Ewes guard and protect the young ones closely for around two weeks, then pay less and less attention to them. By this time the frisky lambs are quite active, and can run as fast as their mothers. With their small size and short horns the ewes are poor fighters, and running gives the lambs a better chance to escape than "freezing" in place, especially since there is little chance to hide in the open areas.

In the wild, argalis live about 12 years. After rutting season is over the older males are weak, and many may die of cold or starvation during the coming winter. Others fall prey to wolves. Few wild animals of any kind ever die of old age.

The World's Longest Horns

Marco Polo sheep (*Ovis ammon poli*) are a subspecies of argali. They are not quite as large as Siberian argalis, but their horns are longer. The world's record for the longest horns of any wild animal, 190.5 centimeters, is held by a Marco Polo sheep. The horns of these animals curve in a wide, open sweep with the two long, slender tips standing far out from the animal's head.

Poli sheep have a rather pale grayish-brown coat with a creamy-white face, underparts, and rump patch. A darker, broad stripe runs from elbow to flank. In winter the animals have a white bib and a thick cape of long hair on the back of the neck. They live on the "roof of the world," the Russian Pamir Plateau, which is made up of great, flattened valleys higher than Pike's Peak.

Although Marco Polo first told the world about these almost mythical animals over 700 years ago, he was not the first westerner to learn about them. Father William, a Franciscan Friar, had reported seeing them close to 20 years earlier. Marco Polo said the Pamir plain where they lived was a desert that took 12 days to ride across, and the great sheep on it had unbelievably long horns. He added that the shepherds made food bowls from the horns, and also used them in constructing cattle pens. The horns are ivory-colored and slender, and weigh little more than half as much as those of the giant Siberian argalis.

No one believed these wild stories until nearly 600 years had passed and a western scientist rediscovered the creatures. A few years later an explorer caught a pair of Marco Polo sheep and took them to England. When the animals had been studied they were named for the great traveler. His tall tale was true after all.

The Smallest Sheep

The mouflon (*Ovis musimon*) is the smallest of all wild sheep. Males are not much larger than collies but are slightly heavier. Mouflons have a beautiful coat of rich chestnut brown with splashes of white and tan, and black markings on the legs. A ruff about the throat, which is quite heavy in winter, is also white, tan, and black.

For hundreds of years true wild mouflons have lived only on the islands of Corsica and Sardinia, just west of Italy. Those found in Europe today were brought in from the islands. Populations of these sheep are found in mountain areas of the islands, where rocks form a jumbled mass. Not many of them are left, and these live in preserves that are poorly protected. Tall heather and thick growths of woody plants help furnish these small creatures with shelter and protection against enemies.

Mouflons graze on grass when they can find it, and are fond of buds and shoots of bushes and young trees, but

The mouflon, smallest of the wild sheep, has a coat of chestnut brown with patches of white and tan. For protection they rely chiefly on their particularly sharp sight.

they will readily eat any plant that is available, from mistletoe to mushrooms. Mouflons have even been known to eat poisonous plants, such as the deadly nightshade, without seeming to come to any harm.

Mouflons have a very good sense of smell, and can hear and respond to sounds some distance away but, as in other sheep, sight is the most important of their senses. They have been known to discover hunters in a blind, and to recognize camouflaged hunters when they were still some distance away. The Corsicans have a saying, "A hair lost by a hunter is heard by a deer, smelled by a boar, and seen by a mouflon ram."

When they are disturbed the animals give a warning whistle and stamp loudly with a front leg. The sound is like a hiss, and is probably uttered through the nose. Ewes often bleat when alarmed, especially if they are searching for a lost lamb. The "ba-a-ah" that answers the mother's bleat sounds like that of any other lamb. Except for a few grunts sometimes heard from old males, rams do most of their noisemaking by banging their horns against rocks or tree trunks, again and again. This seems to be a "Keep Off!" signal, although secretions from the eye glands may also be used as markers.

Lambs stay with the mother for the first year, but are chased off by the ewe when she is ready to give birth again. Newborn lambs double their weight within three weeks and become mature when they are about one and a half years old. Mouflons live from seven to eight years but one old ram broke the record by living for 16 years.

Red Rams

Urials, or red sheep, are much like mouflons in several ways. They are but slightly larger in size, have widely swept back horns and noticeable neck ruffs, and they rarely range high enough in the hills and mountains to get above timber line. Urials are found in scattered groups from the Mediterranean Sea to northern India.

The Elburz urial (*Ovis occidentalis*) is considered to be typical of the group. These animals are long-legged and lean, with red-brown bodies and thick white neck ruffs that hang as a fringe from each cheek. They are found in the Elburz Mountains of northeastern Iran. Like other wild sheep of Asia, urials are better runners than climbers, and can take off at a moment's notice, often hidden by a cloud of dust flipped up by their flying feet.

Much of the land where Iranian urials live is protected mountain pasture. Prince Abdorreza, brother of the Shah of Iran, is an international big game hunter and conservationist, and is interested in seeing that wild sheep have a safe home range. The plentiful supply of food that is present may be part of the reason the animals are so large. It may also help explain why two out of three of the well-fed ewes give birth to twins.

Shy Island Urials

The Cyprus urial (*Ovis occidentalis ophion*), on the island of Cyprus in the Mediterranean, is the smallest and most primitive of all this group. Its sickle-shaped horns, which are about as long as the animal is tall, have very little curl. Cyprus urials have a brown coat with a black, rather small throat mane, and a light gray saddle across the shoulders.

These sheep live in rugged, forested hill country near the eastern end of the island. Much of it is covered with evergreen dwarf oak, and is high, dry, and hot. The desert-like plants provide poor food. The small sheep are sturdy and active, but shy, and will disappear swiftly if one tries to come near. Not many Cyprus urials are left, and the race faces extinction.

Punjab Urials of Pakistan

Punjab urials (*Ovis orientalis punjabiensis*) are said to be the reddest of all wild sheep. They live in northern

Pakistan, in mountain ranges just southwest of the famed Khyber Pass, where much of the land is turning to desert. Forests are gone, and also a great deal of the wildlife. Lions, tigers, swamp deer, and the big one-horned rhinoceros have vanished. A few cheetahs and wild asses, and fewer than 2000 Punjab urials still survive.

Adult male urials usually live in bachelor herds but in October, when it is nearing time for the rut to begin, they grow restless. With neck ruffs looking like black velvet and coppery coats sleek and shiny, the rams prance about at this time as if they know they are handsome. One by one each leaves the herd and roams about alone, looking for a group of females.

Each ewe is sniffed and nuzzled in turn until the ram finds one that is in heat. Then he stays close beside her, strutting stiff-legged and seeming to dare any other male to come near. Sometimes he kicks the female with his foreleg, then chases her madly when she races off. Both may halt and graze quietly before the courtship is continued, but he keeps a wary eye on her.

If a rival shows interest, and the ram can neither scare him off nor stare him down, a fierce fight is likely to follow. The two males trot off in opposite directions, then wheel about and stand tense for an instant before they charge. They run on all four feet, and hurl themselves so hard at each other that their hind legs fly into the air and the crack of their horns raises echoes.

Only a victor can mate with a ewe. As a result, all the lambs born the next spring will have had the biggest, strongest rams as fathers. With a good inheritance like this they are much better able to endure life on these barren hills. Yet in spite of this, many die young.

Ewes go off alone to hidden valleys to give birth. Probably because of the poor food, most of the newborn lambs are weak and thin, and twins are rare. By the next year fewer than half of the lambs will still be alive, but these are the hardiest ones. Frail and feeble lambs never live long enough to pass their weaknesses on to offspring.

A Plan of Action

George B. Schaller, an outstanding zoologist, has made several trips since 1950 to study the Punjab urials. He says that two things are needed if these tough, colorful sheep are to be saved: they must have more rangeland, and more freedom from human interference. Not only must hunters be kept away, but also herdsmen and farmers who, each year, take over more and more of the poor mountain land.

Before any plan of action to save the wild sheep can be decided upon, their habits and behavior need to be known. These can be learned only by months of close study of the animals themselves. It would be useless, for example, to set aside land for the use of the sheep only to find out that for some reason they either could not or would not use it. Also, if domestic sheep and goats are to be kept from crowding wild sheep out, the owners must have some other means of supplying food to their own animals.

Studies such as Schaller's cannot furnish all the answers, but they can be a great help in pointing the way to what must be done.

9

Bighorns Across the Land Bridge

Close to 9000 years ago a big ram with spreading horns climbed and jumped over rubble and rocks, and slushy mounds of ice left by a melting glacier. He was high on the eastern side of the Rocky Mountains in Canada, near the place where two mountain streams joined to form what we now call the Peace River. The great mass of ice over which the ram traveled was riddled with pits and tunnels. Streams of meltwater poured off its surface, and jagged blocks of cracked and crumbling ice barred the ram's path.

Suddenly he fell. Perhaps he crashed through thin ice into a cold, white cavern in the glacier. Or he might have missed his footing on the slippery surface and plunged into a chasm, where he became trapped between walls of ice. Whatever happened, he met his death.

Flood waters from the melting glacier, carrying rocks and rubbish, surged and swirled about the ram's body, and dumped debris on it. After a while the softer parts decayed and disappeared. Bones became separated from one another and some were washed away, but the heavy skull and horns remained. Snows fell and froze, and melted. Centuries passed.

Not many years ago scientists found the long-buried ram's head, far below the surface in a gravel pit. Both skull and horns were in good condition, although a few teeth were missing or broken. In 1972, after the head had been studied, the discovery was reported. Samples of the horn core had been taken to laboratories of the Geological Survey of Canada to be dated, so scientists would know how old the skull was. They found the big ram had made his last climb in the Rockies a little over 9000 years ago.

Snow Sheep of Siberia

Long before the ram died, his ancestors had crossed the Bering Strait land bridge to North America. Scientists believe these ancestors were closely related to the snow sheep which still live in northern Siberia, for these sheep resemble American sheep much more than they do the other sheep of Asia. Unlike argalis, mouflons, and urials, they are stocky and short-legged, with broad chests and massive shoulders and hips.

American sheep and snow sheep can jump and climb as ibexes do, and are just as likely to bound up steep cliffs or stroll along the edge of a precipice. The tails are broad and dark, not light and thin as are those of Asian sheep, and the eye-gland is a half-moon-shaped fold of skin instead of a straight slit. Secretions from it do not run out and streak the face.

Several races of snow sheep are known. Kamchatka snow sheep (*Ovis nivicola*) live in the most eastern part of Siberia. The males are larger than any of the urial sheep, but are neither as tall nor as heavy as the big argalis. Females are much smaller. The long, shaggy coat is a grizzled gray-brown, with the head and neck lighter. Usually there is a dark patch on the face. The ears are quite small, as is the rump patch at the base of the tail.

Horns of Kamchatka sheep are not heavy but they are usually a little longer than the animal is tall. Tips spread widely outward, even when the lower part of the curl is close to the cheeks. The horn tips are delicate and sharp, but are rarely damaged. All snow sheep, because of their light-weight horns, are known as Asian thinhorns.

Scientists who have studied snow sheep say that males, during the rutting season, stride about with head held high and horns on display. If a rival appears, an old ram will probably try to stare him down, or use a front kick on him. Sometimes he will attempt to mount the rival as he does females, or males of lower rank. Usually one or the other gives in and leaves without a real fight.

Snow sheep live in the highlands on rough, rugged ground, but the forage is good, and newborn lambs are well developed and healthy. Their woolly coats are ash to dark gray at first, but these are shed in early fall and the still small sheep take on the look of adults. Snow sheep may live for ten or twelve years or more. The record, reported in 1967, is 18 years.

Sheep That Braved the Glaciers

Sheep from Asia are thought to have reached North America between 200,000 and 100,000 years ago. For thousands of years they roamed over the tundra of Beringia and the central part of the land that is now Alaska. The rest of the continent was closed to them, shut off by immense glaciers on the north, east, and south.

The next to the last of the great ice sheets crept so far southward that a bulge at its front edge reached down to what is now southern Illinois. When this huge glacier began to melt back toward the north about 100,000 years ago, long tongues of ice were left on the mountain ranges, but river valleys and low places between mountains became ice-free. Passageways to the east and south opened up.

One of these was a corridor on the eastern side of the Rockies. Grazing herds from Alaska made their way into it and slowly drifted southward and eastward over North America; but no goats or sheep, or any of their relatives, ever went as far south as South America.

Several "little ice ages" occurred during the long warmer period before the final great glacier advanced toward the south. Smaller ice sheets edged forward and spread over northern lands, choking valleys. Many creatures perished, but a few members of the goat-sheep subfamily braved the blizzards and blinding snow storms, and found pockets of pasture and shelter.

Sheep were able to cross over Beringia for a few more thousand years, before this last ice-age glacier began to melt. Finally, as the glacier shrank northward, the corridor from Alaska was opened again. The sea level rose higher and higher from the floods of meltwater, and the wide plains that had been Beringia now became sea bottom again. For the last six to eight thousand years Asia and North America have been separated by a wide channel of water, and animals can no longer cross from one continent to another.

Groups of sheep, cut off from the other herds, began to develop differently. Some of the separated groups became enough unlike the others that several races were formed. One of the best known of these is the Dall sheep (*Ovis dalli*), sometimes called the Alaska white sheep.

Great White Sheep

Dall sheep are beautiful animals. The whole body is creamy white except for a few dark hairs that sometimes grow along the spine and tail. Nostrils and lips are black, and hoofs and horns are a light golden amber in color, The eyes are a gold bronze, and have the black, slitlike pupils that are common to sheep and goats. Dall sheep are about the same size as snow sheep, but the horns are longer. Like those of snow sheep, the horns are slender and light in weight and the tips flare widely, although the lower part of the curl is usually close to the cheek. The different races of Dall sheep are known as American thinhorns.

During the summer the sheep live high on the mountains, usually close to cliffs. Ewes and lambs form large herds, but the rams either group into small herds or live alone. All have keen eyesight and can easily catch the scent of a human being. Sudden danger can put the whole group into action in an instant, and they bolt to safety.

Sometimes, instead of running, alarmed Dall sheep move away at a rigid, tense walk, usually going uphill. After a few feet they may stop to look back at whatever disturbed them. One band of sheep, surprised by a lone wolf, first started to leave, then walked about the wolf in a stiff, tight circle, watching him. Finally the entire herd lay down, facing the wolf, and stared at it silently. This seemed to be too much for the animal and it soon trotted off.

Black Thinhorns

Stone sheep (*Ovis dalli stonei*) are a more southern race of Dall sheep that live in northwestern Canada, north of the Peace River. These animals range from grizzled gray to a glossy blue-black, but all have a lighter patch between the horns. Muzzle and rump patch are white, and each leg has a white streak on the back. A dark stripe runs from the spine through the rump patch and on to the black tail.

The creamy white Dall sheep are excellent climbers and jumpers; these abilities, along with keen senses of sight and smell, are effective defenses.

Rocky Mountain bighorn sheep are large, sturdy animals found in Canada and down as far as New Mexico.

Horns of Stone rams are brownish-amber in color and are usually somewhat longer and heavier than those of Dall sheep. One twelve-year-old black ram in British Columbia had unusually long horns. They curled in closely toward his cheeks, then flared out so widely that a person with hands clasped on his chest, and elbows held out from his body, could lean between the tips, with room to spare.

Thinhorns of America are still much like their relatives in Siberia, the snow sheep, but the groups of American sheep that drifted down the corridor east of the Rockies have become changed in a number of ways. Over the years they have developed into several races which we call the bighorns.

America's Mountain Sheep

Rocky Mountain bighorns (*Ovis canadensis*) are found in a broad area from central British Columbia in Canada, south of the Peace River, down into northern New Mexico and westward into Idaho and Utah. These are large, magnificent animals, second only to the giant argalis of Siberia. Their huge, heavy horns curve close to the cheeks, with the tips pointing slightly outward, and the largest ones curl to make more than the first coil of a spiral.

Mountain sheep are almost as active and sure-footed as ibexes or other wild goats. They scramble up slopes, zigzag along narrow ledges, and find footing on steep, high cliffs. When storms come they find shelter in caves or under overhanging rocks.

Since 1961 Dr. Valerius Geist of the University of Calgary, in Canada, has spent much time finding out about the behavior of bighorns and thinhorns of North America. His study area for Rocky Mountain bighorns was in Banff National Park, on the eastern side of the Rockies in southern Alberta. Although this land is wilderness, human beings have interfered more than once. Wolves were poisoned out twice, and a large artificial lake was created when a power dam was built. Bison once lived there, but now are extinct in that area. The sheep live in open grassy or rocky regions, above the forests.

Geist studied three populations of sheep on three mountains. Each group had several home ranges, and moved to one or the other of these at special times of the year. The ranges were linked by sheep trails, and sometimes were a great distance apart.

Sex, Size, and Rank

Geist soon found that the sheep more or less divide themselves into classes that are based on sex, body size, and horn size. The youngest group, newborn lambs to those about six months old, all look alike whether they are male or female; differences develop gradually.

By two and one-half years of age the females have become fully adult, and are able to bear young. They seem to change but little after this, for the rest of their lives. The young rams, however, are now half a head taller than the females, and their horns have begun the downward curl. These rams are now "teen-agers," not yet fully grown although larger than their mothers.

Horns are symbols of rank, and rams act according to their horn size. When two rams meet, each one seems to size up the other. One of them is then likely to give the other a front kick, sometimes with a low growl, or to go up to the other displaying his horns, with head lowered and ears laid back. The secondary ram may admit he is inferior by some action such as turning his back to the bigger ram, or licking the other's face. Otherwise, a fight is on.

On one occasion an old ram with huge horns, one of which was badly broken, met a five-year-old ready to fight. The old ram lowered his head and laid back his ears, but turned his head so that the broken horn showed. The five-year-old was fooled. He looked the older ram over, then walked up and kicked him squarely in the chest. The fight was on—but it was soon over. After one whirling, furious charge by the old ram, the younger one at once began to lick the other's face, and to show he thoroughly understood he was lower in rank.

Sex Behavior Patterns

A high-ranking or dominant ram treats other smaller sheep alike, whether they are male or female. He may use the front kick to prove his rank, stretch out his neck with lowered head, display his horns, or threaten to fight. As a final test he mounts the smaller sheep as if it were a female in heat.

All younger males, and females in heat, react to the ram in the same way. They let him kick, or mount, or do as he wishes. In addition they may lick or nuzzle his face, or rub his face, neck or shoulders. When younger rams thus admit they are lower in rank, they are allowed to stay with the herd instead of being chased off. This behavior is probably helpful to the group, for young, inexperienced animals that had to live alone would more easily be killed by predators.

Rams are sometimes said to be homosexual because they so often mount smaller rams of the same sex, and the younger allow it, but this conclusion is not strictly correct. Homosexual individuals prefer to be with members of their own sex, and leave the opposite sex alone. Rams do not do this. They will follow a female in heat anytime instead of a younger male, and often are so keenly interested that they may not eat for days. The mounting of another male seems to be simply one of several ways of saying "I'm the boss." Compared with humans, four-footed animals have only a limited number of ways in which they can make statements.

Females that are not in heat act much like yearlings. They jump away from a nosing, curious male and run off. Ewes rarely fight among themselves, but one may butt or threaten another, or chase a smaller one away. Sheep of either sex pay little attention to juveniles, other than to butt them out of the way if their playfulness interferes with what the older animals are doing.

In late October and early November rams begin to join bands of ewes. Male sheep do not collect harems of females, nor do they form breeding territories. Instead, a number of rams gather around a ewe about to come in heat and follow her wherever she goes. Soon the biggest ram begins to try running the others off, and while he is doing this the ewe is likely to grab the chance to run away from him.

A wild chase follows, usually with a younger ram just behind the ewe and the big ram hot on his heels. The ewe may jump off the trail, or turn and back into a crevice in the cliffs, but she finally gives up. The big ram and the ewe may then stay together for several hours or a day or two, and mate a number of times.

Lambs in Bands

Lambs are born in late May or early June. Two or three weeks before this the ewe runs off her yearling lamb, then goes off by herself. Usually she chooses a place with broken, rugged cliffs or high ledges where it would be almost impossible for an enemy to follow. Soon after the lamb is born the ewe licks and cleans it thoroughly. As she noses it, both learn each other's smell.

A few days later mother and lamb return to the herd. Immediately the yearlings, and the barren ewes that did not produce a lamb this year, crowd around the newborn. They seem to be particularly interested when the lamb begins to suckle. Often mother and offspring have to take to their heels to escape the meddlesome onlookers, and allow the young one to nurse in peace.

Within a few weeks the lambs begin to form juvenile bands, and soon they are returning to their mothers only long enough to suckle. The lambs butt, clashing their heads together, mount each other, jump, kick, and paw the ground. Each new trick or game holds high interest for a while, and they do the same thing over and over again. Like all mammals, they learn by playing, and the memories stored then become useful later when the sheep have become adults.

Desert Bighorns

Several races of bighorns are known. One subspecies, the badlands bighorn of the Dakotas and nearby states, became extinct probably half a century or more ago. All the other races live in desert areas in the southwest, and are known as desert bighorns. Probably best known of these is the Nelson bighorn (*Ovis canadensis nelsoni*) which is found in southern Nevada and California. Death Valley, one of the hottest spots on earth, is included in its range.

Desert sheep are smaller than their mountain relatives. The light brown coat, with a reddish-yellow tinge on neck and shoulders, matches their bare, dusty surroundings. Heavy, often tightly curled horns are not quite as large as those of mountain bighorns, but are sometimes more eagerly sought after as trophies by hunters because it is so hard to obtain one. The hoofs are bigger than those of deer, and the toes spread widely, so it is easy for the sheep to walk up slippery rock faces or bound up or down steep cliffs.

Nights are cold on the desert, but the days can be blazing hot, and there is little rainfall. Many desert plants are covered with spines, hooks, or thorns, which help the plants keep their scanty supply of water. Others, such as cacti, store water in their thick stems. Sheep may nibble off small thorns, or batter off larger ones with their horns, and reach the juicy pulp inside.

Rocky Mountain sheep and desert bighorns together once covered most of the western third of the continent. Today over 90 per cent of them are gone. The few thousand now left are remnant herds, found only here and there in isolated pockets.

Much of the loss is due to diseases, especially those brought in by domestic cattle and sheep that, more and more, are taking over grazing lands that wild sheep have used for centuries. One of the worst of the diseases is lungworm infection which is often followed by pneumonia, and complicated with roundworm and itch mite infestations. These last burrow under the skin and produce crusty sores and loss of hair. In some herds as high as 95 per cent of the sick animals have died.

Bighorns need grass, and some means of obtaining water. For thousands of years the wild herds followed old trails, season by season, to winter range, salt lick, lambing area, and summer range. No one region was overgrazed, or destroyed by trampling feet. Each generation, younger rams learned these routes from the old leaders and, in turn, passed the knowledge on.

When great herds of livestock flooded the rangelands in the early 1900s, many grasslands were destroyed, and sagebrush spread. The soil, no longer protected, soon washed away. In 11 western states 80 per cent of the grazing land now grows only sagebrush, scrubby shrubs, and weeds.

Head-Hunting

Trophy-hunting also takes its toll of bighorns. This sport was begun officially in the late 1800s when Theodore Roosevelt founded the Boone and Crockett Club. Its aim was to promote both conservation of big game animals and "manly sport with the rifle." At that time there were many sheep, but few hunters, and most of those who did hunt had high principles regarding the sport. Today almost the opposite is true. Head-hunting has become big business.

Trophy poaching rings have been uncovered in several states. These rings have included taxidermists, businessmen, and even an aviation company. The fine for taking a sheep illegally is about $300 to $500, but a poacher can sell a head for $3000 to $5000 and up. One sale can thus pay for a large number of fines. Changing laws would probably not stop black market profits completely, but they would help. What is needed is changed attitudes.

Many sportsmen who are honestly interested in preserving wildlife urge that rewards for needless killing be stopped. This would include no publishing of pictures or articles honoring some kill, no awards of pins or patches, and no further registration of animals in record books. They suggest camera-hunting instead.

One who loves the tangy freshness and spiciness of an early morning in the woods or mountains, or is excited by the thrill of the chase or delights in the skill needed for stalking prey and capturing it, could find the same satisfaction and exhilaration holding a camera instead of a gun. He could bring home more than just a memory of a living animal beside a rock or stream, yet not have to cut down some stately creature in the prime of life and leave it a bloody mess.

A trophy that is only a glassy-eyed head on a wall will, in time, become dusty and moth-eaten. On the other hand, a series of true-to-life photographs of a magnificent animal would qualify as a distinguished prize anywhere. They could be displayed proudly, and would last indefinitely.

Bighorns or Burros?

In addition to disease, livestock, and hunters, bighorns face another problem in the form of hardy, lovable, floppy-eared burros. Abandoned by early prospectors who died or gave up the search for gold, these rugged, appealing creatures have made the wild lands their home. With no enemies to keep them in check, they have multiplied enormously.

Thousands of burros have destroyed much of the range on which sheep and other native animals depend. Not enough food is left in many places to support both bighorns and burros. In Death Valley, for example, where 5000 native bighorns once lived, fewer than 600 are found there now, and the number steadily decreases. By contrast, over 1500 burros live in Death Valley. They are rapidly running out of space even for themselves, for they are able to double their population every four years.

In areas where burros grew to be too numerous, the extra ones were shot for many years, and the animals thus kept under control. Recently, however, many people who knew nothing of the problems that too many burros could cause raised an uproar. They demanded that all killing of burros be stopped immediately. Now, according to law, anyone who disturbs a burro faces the penalty of a $2000 fine or a year in jail, or both. The fine for killing one of our few native sheep illegally is still only $300 to $500.

The disappearing bighorns are native only in North America, but burros are found all over the world. There is food for both in the canyons and hills if the burros are kept under control. If they are not, it will be the native animal that perishes. When bighorns are gone, it will be forever.

10

The Meekest Animal

No one really knows which were domesticated first, goats or sheep, but the oldest bones found so far belong to sheep. In the Zagros Mountains, in northern Iraq, 11,000-year-old sheep bones have been dug up at the Shanidar site. Studies show that by that time sheep had probably been living with humans, under their protection, for many years.

From the beginning, sheep have been among our most useful animals. They provided not only tasty meat, and skins and wool for clothing, but also played a role in many religions. People offering sacrifices to the gods often preferred sheep, especially lambs, above all other animals. These mild-mannered animals were looked upon as harmless, innocent creatures. At festivals, songs were sung that praised the meek and sacred lamb. Even today, lambs are sometimes carved on children's tombstones as a symbol of innocence.

Sheep were also used more than any other animal for divination, or foretelling the future. Priests cut the animal open and examined such organs as the heart, lungs, kidneys, and intestines, according to strict rules. Most important was the liver. The appearance of each part of this organ was thought to be related in some way to the affairs of the king or the country. Young apprentices were taught to "divine" or interpret these signs.

Domestic sheep (*Ovis aries*) are very different from their wild relatives, especially in having thick, woolly coats instead of long, sparser ones. Probably some of the early farmers or sheepherders noticed that some of their tamed animals had more wool than others, just as some of the wild ones do today. If the owners kept such animals, and bred them and their woolliest offspring, there is a good chance they could finally obtain sheep that had less ordinary hair and a great deal more wool. This would be a long process, and would require many generations of sheep.

Wool Empires

Woollen goods have been important for thousands of years, but Spain was the first nation to produce a special breed of wool-bearing sheep. About 800 years ago sheep-owners in that country developed a new breed with such unusually fine wool that, even today, it is considered to be of the highest quality. These Merino sheep soon became so valuable that, according to Spanish law, anyone who sold a single ewe out of the country was sentenced to death. Money for the voyages of Columbus, and those of later explorers, came from the wool trade.

Although Merino sheep were jealously guarded for centuries, in 1786 Spain finally sold nearly 400 ewes to the King of France. He crossed the animals with rams on his own estate at Rambouillet, and produced another new breed, the Rambouillet. Today these sheep are second only to Merinos in producing fine wool.

England's wool empire began over 2000 years ago. When Julius Caesar's soldiers raided Britain during the first century B.C., they found great herds of sheep, and a wool industry already started. About 500 years ago wool was so important to England that, by law, no one was allowed either to buy wool from another country or sell it to them. Another law stated that each person over seven years old had to wear a wool cap when he went out of doors, or he would be fined 80 cents each time he was caught.

Nearly 200 years later King Henry VIII seized flocks from monasteries and certain other private owners throughout the country, and gave them to his favorites. The new owners fenced the sheep in, and shepherds and weavers all over the land had no way left to make a living. Those who could not pay their debts were then thrown in prison. Many of the immigrants to the new colonies in America were shepherds and weavers from debtors' prisons.

Early colonists were forbidden by the English to have any sheep at all. Many of the settlers felt the king's orders were not fair, and smuggled sheep into the country. By the end of the seventeenth century colonists were shipping wool to other countries, and the English were so furious they passed a law saying that anyone caught trading in sheep or wool would have his right hand cut off. Colonists were soon up in arms. This unreasonable law, together with the Stamp Act and several other unjust actions, helped bring about the American Revolution.

Spanish Merinos

Both George Washington and Thomas Jefferson wore suits of American wool when they were inaugurated. Both knew that even our best wool was not as fine as that of France or Spain, so they did all they could to help farmers obtain better wool-bearing sheep. Finally, just after the turn of the century, Spain agreed to sell some Merinos to

The Merino sheep with its thickly bunched fleece on many folds of skin is virtually a living wool factory. It has played a part in providing foundation stock for a number of other breeds. A good Merino ram for breeding costs many thousands of dollars.

the United States. By 1811 we had about 29,000 fine wool-producing sheep.

The first of these Merinos were shipped to us by the United States Minister to Spain. They sold in the States for about $1500 each. A few years earlier a farmer by the name of Foster is said to have smuggled into the country a flock of sheep which accidentally included three Merinos. He had no idea how valuable the animals were, and had them butchered. For a while Foster ate some very costly meals.

Good Merinos, especially rams that are to be used for breeding, are much more expensive today. The highest price ever paid for a sheep of any kind was $36,000 in Australian money, which would have been equal to $52,800 in United States money. The sheep was a Merino ram, and was bought by F. L. Puckridge of South Australia.

Merino sheep are medium-sized animals that are well suited to living under range conditions, even when the country is rugged and somewhat dry. Compared to meat-producing sheep, Merinos can get along with little feed, water, or shelter. The fleece is heavy and soft, with well-crimped fibers, and it grows on the legs down to the tops of the hoofs. Wool clipped from a good ram at one shearing could be spun into a thread long enough to reach from St. Louis to the Gulf of Mexico.

Rambouillet sheep, sometimes called the French Merino, is the only other breed that is raised primarily for its wool. These animals are large and hardy, and also do well under range conditions. Rambouillet wool is a little coarser than that from Merinos, but the fleece is fine and heavy, and the breed is quite popular because the animals are easy to herd. These sheep have a strong flocking instinct, and rarely stray far from the main group.

Spring Sheep-Shearing

Sheep are shorn in the springtime soon after the weather becomes warm. Farmers with only a few animals may use large hand or electric clippers much like those of a barber, but large flocks are taken to shearing sheds. Inside are one or more long rows of big clippers run by electric motors. A shearer waits beside each clipper.

Sheep shearers are experts that travel from one part of the country to another as they are needed. One who is experienced can strip a sheep completely in three minutes or less. As each sheep is delivered he holds it between his knees and clips with long, sure strokes, beginning with the legs and belly. The fibers are so matted and tangled that the fleece rolls off in one piece as if it were a blanket.

Sheep-shearing experts are specialists at their trade, and take pride in the speed with which they work. The record at the time of writing is 77 lambs shorn in an hour.

When the shearer turns to the next sheep, a helper rolls up and ties the just-clipped fleece, and places it in a big bag with twenty to forty others. Full bags are pressed into the smallest size possible with a big machine, then are marked so they can be identified and sent to the warehouse or mill. Another helper herds the wriggling, naked sheep into pens where they are counted and marked. Usually they are routed through a bath of medicated water before being set free to run in the pasture again.

Shearers sometimes race each other to see who can clip the most sheep. The record to date was set on June 25, 1975, by G. Phillips, at Tymawr Farms in Wales. In a nine-hour working day, using electric clippers, Phillips sheared 694 lambs. This is an average of about 77 lambs an hour, or less than a minute for each.

Self-Shearing Sheep

A few years ago scientists studying anti-cancer drugs at the Animal Science Research Division of the United States Department of Agriculture, in Beltsville, Maryland, made an interesting discovery. They found that a chemical in the nitrogen-mustard family, which stops growth in cancer cells, would also interfere with the growth of new cells at the roots of hairs in several kinds of animals. High doses would kill, but a dose only about one-fourth as strong as that could be used without harm. It would act on the hair cells within a few hours and, for the most part, would be gone from the body by the next day.

This drug, called CPA for short, kills new cells at the hair roots for only a few hours, if the right dose is given.

Then the hair starts growing again. About a week and a half later the weakened section of hair has been pushed above the skin. This part of the hair is constricted or squeezed in. A jerk, such as one might use to pull adhesive tape from the skin, breaks the hair at this point, and the entire coat can be peeled off easily. The sheep feel no pain. If the hair is allowed to grow for two to three weeks after the drug is given, the weak place will be far enough above the skin surface that a short, woolly layer will cover the animal when it is "peeled."

Fleeces obtained by this method are of high quality. They are a little heavier than normal, and the fibers are somewhat longer. The animals seem to feel no side effects, and fleeces grown the next year are as heavy as usual.

Fleeces are graded at the mill according to how coarse or how fine the fibers are, and how long. Wool fibers are quite different from those of cotton or linen. A single fiber pulled from a piece of woollen cloth or yarn looks like a fine, crinkly hair. It is made of thousands of tiny scales. If a fiber were cut crosswise, and the cut end looked at under a microscope, it would show that the fiber was oval in shape, not round. Oval fibers or hairs bend and curl, but round ones stay straight.

Wool's oval fibers act like minute coiled springs. If they are pulled out of shape, they spring back again. Wool threads twisted together are difficult to pull apart because the crimps and coils hold together tightly. Such fibers also trap and hold air in the spaces, and make a layer of insulation. In the winter this air layer in woollen garments keeps the body warmth inside, and prevents cold air from seeping in.

Second to None

Cloth is made by weaving crosswise threads in and out between threads stretched lengthwise and fastened on a loom. Before the woven cloth is wound on a bolt it is washed, preshrunk with moisture and heat, and pressed. Some fabrics are brushed to give them a fuzzy appearance. Others have the surface clipped or singed so it will be smooth. Sometimes, by applying certain chemicals, cloth is made rainproof, mothproof, or wrinkle-proof. Wool can be dyed at any stage, either as fibers or as woven goods. If the dye is good, the colors will remain bright as long as the cloth lasts.

No other fabric is superior in so many ways. Wool naturally sheds water well and, because of the tiny scales, it does not pick up dirt easily. It can be made into material useful for heavy, warm clothing, or it can be woven into such lightweight cloth that it can be worn as an evening gown. It is tough, not easily torn, and wears well.

Wool is also resistant to fire. With high heat it may smoulder slowly, but it does not burst into flame. There is little danger of a cancer scare such as occurred in 1977 after thousands of children's sleeping garments, made of synthetic material, had been treated to make them resistant to fire. The chemical used had not been tested thoroughly, and later experiments showed it could produce cancer in test animals.

We shall probably never know exactly how long ago humans learned to spin thread or to weave cloth, but the oldest pieces of cloth known so far date back to a long-buried city in Turkey. They were found in the 1960s when archaeologists were digging in the ruins of the forgotten city of Catal Hüyük. Laboratory tests showed the pieces were 7900 years old.

The people of Catal wrapped their dead in cloth, and stuffed the skulls with it also, then buried the bodies under sleeping platforms in houses or shrines. Centuries ago a great fire destroyed the entire city, but no air was able to get inside the tightly-closed graves. As a result, the bodies and their wrappings did not burn, but the terrific heat changed the cloth to carbon. Since this substance does not decay, there was no further change in the cloth's appearance. It is impossible to tell now whether the fibers were of wool, or of cotton or linen, but the charred fragments show clearly that the wrappings were of cloth, carefully woven.

Today synthetic fabrics are used in many ways, and usually cost less than those woven from wool or other natural fibers. Whether or not they are as durable is another question. Wool, though expensive, is still so important that in the United States alone the value of wool fabrics sold each year is well over five million dollars.

11

Food for a Hungry World

Not many sheep make headlines but George, a Suffolk lamb, was an exception. He received an official executive pardon from the governor of Illinois.

In the summer of 1976 George was the grand champion wether at the Illinois State Fair. Later he was sold at auction for $3700. According to state fair regulations, a winning animal must be slaughtered by the following October 15.

George was bought by a restaurant owner in Chicago who expected to serve a big dinner to some of his friends at $400 a plate. However, George had friends, too. A group of outraged third and fourth graders, with the help of Save-A-Pet, Inc., got busy. After several dozen letters and phone calls, the governor agreed to grant a pardon. George's life was saved; he now lives at Lincoln Park Zoo, Chicago.

George's forebears came from England, as did those of many other breeds of sheep. In fact, sheep have had a long history in America. Columbus himself, on his second voyage, brought the first band of sheep to the New World, along with a few goats and cattle.

Later ships brought more of these animals, as well as horses, hogs, and hens. Soon a number of royal ranches were set up with certain of the king's friends in charge. Indians at first were terrified by these odd animals with their strange sounds, for they had never seen such creatures before.

As colonists poured into the new country they brought

more farm animals. Always there were large flocks of sheep. A century later many grasslands in both North and South America were covered with thousands of grazing sheep. These shy domesticated animals were far different from the wild bighorns of the western plains.

Conquistadors, who explored new lands and raided Indians in their search for gold, always took meat animals on their journeys, and the favorite was sheep. These sturdy creatures could find food where cattle would starve. Coronado started his quest for the fabled Seven Cities of Gold with only a few hundred hogs and cattle, but he included five thousand sheep.

One or more priests went along with every explorer. According to law, the ownership of all new lands was decided by the Pope. He gave control over all the New World to Ferdinand and Isabella, the King and Queen of Spain, on the condition that the natives were to be Christianized. Priests, usually Franciscan friars, were sent to the new land to set up missions and see that this was done.

Two centuries later over one hundred missions had been started. They covered much of the land in New Mexico and California, and regions in between. Friars at each mission had to be pioneer shepherds and wool-growers, for the missions depended on their flocks of sheep for both food and clothing. Later, whatever ruler happened to be in charge at the time took over most of the mission property and turned it into private ranches.

Meat on the Hoof

When the great gold rush began in the middle of the nineteenth century, the hordes of men who rushed westward needed food. Sheep provided an answer. Tens of thousands of sheep trudged dusty trails for days to reach the mining camps.

At first the animals sold for $1 a head, but the price soon rose to between $15 and 25. One old sheepman who could not count made sure that he got all that was due him by stationing himself at the cutting gate where the sheep filed in, one by one. As each animal skittered past he made the buyer drop a silver dollar in his hat.

Today about 200 breeds of sheep are known, but this number would be doubled if all the varieties of each breed were counted. There are sheep of all kinds: tall and short, fat and lean, fat-tailed, short-tailed, lop-eared, without ears, well filled out, or with sagging folds of skin. Many sheep have two horns, others have none, and some breeds in certain northern islands grow four or even eight horns. Tibetan unicorn sheep have only one horn. There is at least one breed for every kind of pasture and for most climates.

Most of these breeds are raised as meat-producers, but their wool is sold too. It is of good quality, although the fibers are coarser and shorter than those of Merino or Rambouillet sheep. This wool is useful for all kinds of ordinary clothing.

Lambs to Market

Sheep are reared in all states, but the great flocks are in the West. Many sheepmen have from 1000 to 10,000 sheep. About 17 million lambs are born each year, and most of these go to market. Enough lamb is eaten in the United States to provide each person with about 16 or 17 good meals.

Sheep dogs not only round up herds but also find and protect lost sheep. Some herds number up to 10,000.

Spring lambs usually spend the first summer with their mothers in high mountain pastures. Before the first snowfall they are moved down to lower pastures, and the owner then decides which lambs he wants to keep for breeding ewes. The others are sold.

Some of the lambs go straight to a packing house. Others are brought by "feeders" who fatten the lambs further, then sell them when they are about nine months old. Wethers are often fattened for another year until they are close to 20 months old. Their meat is sold as mutton.

Most of the more common breeds are known as medium-wool types. George, the officially pardoned lamb, is a dark-face Suffolk sheep of the medium-wool type. This is a rugged breed that produces excellent meat, but the wool is of rather poor quality. Suffolks can stand a lot of heat, and are often grown under range conditions. Hampshires are dark-face sheep that are quite popular in the United States, as are also Southdowns, Shropshires, and Oxfords. Southdowns are used all over the world as meat-producers.

Sausages and Surgeons

Although sheep are raised mainly for their meat or wool, other products obtained from them are also valuable. Organs such as the liver, heart, and kidneys are used for human food, and medicines are made from some of the glands. Insulin, obtained from one of the digestive glands, is so necessary to people who have diabetes that they may die without it.

The intestines are used for sausage casings, and for "catgut" strings that are put to good use in both medicine and music. Surgeons use catgut to sew up cuts after operations, and strings in violins and other musical instruments are made from it. Leather made from the skin of sheep is used for shoes, gloves, book bindings, and covers of chairs and couches.

Sheep grease, which is washed out when wool is cleaned, is separated from the dirt and water, and purified. It is then known as lanolin, and it forms the base for many cosmetics and beauty aids, from lipstick to hand cream. Fat from the meat is made into candles. Glue and fertilizer are manufactured from waste parts such as hoofs. Almost nothing is lost.

Some sheep are grown for neither wool nor meat, but mainly for their pelts. The small, hardy Karakul sheep of central Asia produce beautiful lambskin fur. Coat fibers in most of the newborn lambs are glossy black and form a "watery" pattern of short, tight curls. The small lambs are skinned when they are one to three days old, and the fur is sold as broadtail or Persian lamb.

Some Karakul lambs are born with gray fur. These fibers are often somewhat coarser than the black ones, but they lie in shiny, open curls. Gray fur pelts, commonly sold as caracul or astrakhan, are also made into expensive fur or fur-trimmed garments.

Karakul lamb is good to eat, but mutton from the adults is of poor grade. Sheared wool is also low in quality. The fibers are dark and coarse, and wiry outer fibers are mixed with the softer ones of the undercoat. This wool is used for carpets, but little else.

Sheep milk is unknown to most people, but in some European areas sheep are raised as triple-purpose animals, and milk ranks with meat and wool as an important product. The East Friesian milk sheep of Germany are considered to be one of the best breeds, but the La Razza Sarda of Sardinia are also valued highly because, in addition to being heavy milk producers, the animals have a long, white fleece. Milk sheep are also raised in Balkan countries and in the region of France where Roquefort cheese is made.

Like goats, sheep are sometimes put to odd uses. In Bonn, West Germany, a young student decided to earn her way through college with the help of 300 sheep which she advertised as "woollen lawnmowers." Schools, factories, homeowners, and even a helicopter landing field paid for the services of the "cleanest, quietest, and most nonpolluting lawnmower one can get." Rent-A-Sheep was so successful that the young student announced in 1976 she planned to increase her lawnmower flock to 700.

Long before Mary had a little lamb, sheep made charming pets, but two-year-old Roger, in Lake Dallas, Texas, added a new twist. Each evening he joined his owners on their patio for a daily ration of vodka sours. Roger sampled his first glassful a year earlier, and came back for more. His owners report that he handled it well.

Pastures and Parasites

All over the world are vast stretches of somewhat dry grazing land that is ideal for many breeds of sheep. The world sheep population is around one billion, with Australia and the Soviet Union leading with the greatest numbers of animals. In the northwestern part of South Australia is the largest sheep station or ranch in the world. Close to 90,000 sheep are raised here, along with about 700 cattle. Several thousand native kangaroos also make themselves at home in the pastures.

One problem common to all sheep growers is disease. As a group, sheep seem to suffer more from parasites than any other farm or ranch animal. Usually the lambs and younger animals are the ones most harmed. Worm parasites that cause a great deal of damage include flukes, tapeworms, and roundworms.

One of the worst is the liver fluke. This parasite may grow to be nearly as wide as one's little finger, and half as long, and have a complicated life history much like that of the stomach flukes of goats. Certain medicines help get rid of the flukes, but giving the medicine to enormous flocks of sheep is almost impossible. The only real solution to this difficulty is to destroy all snails which can carry one of the larval stages, but this is not easy.

Skin infections, often brought about by small crawling creatures such as lice, ticks, and scab mites, are especially bad in sheep because this lowers the value of the wool. Most of these external parasites can be controlled if the sheep are dipped completely, even to covering the head for an instant, in cool water that has the proper chemical in it. This, too, is a long, tiring process when thousands of sheep have to be dipped.

Problems with Predators

In a number of areas the biggest problem is what to do about animals that prey on the sheep. All predators, from bears and wolves to roving packs of dogs, will kill sheep when they are hungry, just as they would any other food animal, but few are steady sheep-killers. When sheep are slain it is usually because thousands of them are handy, and are easy to run down, while well-hidden wild creatures that are much fewer in number have to be hunted.

Lambs are especially open to attack. Much of the loss of quite young lambs occurs because the ewes so often leave the protection of the flock and find some out-of-the-way place to give birth. Lambs do not fight, and it is not difficult for a strong, hungry predator to outwit the ewe and grab the lamb.

The Hated Coyote

Of all the creatures that prey on flocks, coyotes are probably the most hated. Over the years, as more and more forests and plains were taken over by farmers and ranchmen, wolves, cougars, and most other predators retreated farther into the wilderness. They became fewer in number, and in many places were wiped out entirely. Not so the coyote. It simply adapted to humans' ways and learned to live in spite of them.

Biologists who have studied predators say that only a few coyotes, like certain human criminals, are "bad guys" and seem to kill for the fun of it. Most coyotes do not hunt unless they are hungry, and then take only enough for themselves and their pups. As predators, they are a necessary link in natural life cycles. Under normal conditions they feed mainly on mice, rabbits, and other small creatures that eat food crops. They also serve as scavengers by devouring dead animals.

It is true that sheep-raisers face a problem in that the sheep industry has been going steadily downhill for the last 20 years or more. In 1961 over 32,700,000 sheep were raised in the United States, but twelve years later the number was only a little over 17,700,000. This decline cannot be due to coyotes, however, for it is greater in the eastern states, where few or no coyotes are found.

There are many reasons that the sheep industry finds itself in trouble. People have learned to like the taste of beef, and eat more of it. They buy synthetic materials for clothes instead of the more expensive wool and cotton. Costs of raising sheep have risen enormously, especially in wages paid to shepherds.

As a result, great flocks are commonly left alone on mountain pastures with no one to look after or protect them. Untended sheep can get into all sorts of trouble. Some become victims of falls or snake-bite, or eat poisonous weeds. Lambs may die of exposure. Sheep-stealing is widespread. Many shepherds, however, report most of their losses as due to coyotes without trying to find the real cause.

Those who raise sheep insist that they must poison, trap, or shoot all coyotes if they are to save their sheep and make a profit, but this is questionable. There can be no excuse whatever for a widespread and careless use of such tools of death. Innocent animals, and even pets and people, have been killed by them. Usually only the less intelligent coyotes are caught, however, for the smarter, craftier ones soon learn how to avoid all these devices and teach their young to do the same.

Ringing bells, electric shocks, and bad tastes and smells have also been used to drive off predators. These worked for a while, but the animals soon paid little attention to them. In fact, no kind of control ever tried has, so far, really protected sheep without the presence of a good shepherd.

Some biologists are hopeful about the use of poison collars. Since coyotes take their prey by grabbing the throat, an attacker would be killed outright. The big advantage of this method is that only the individual coyote bent on killing a sheep would become a victim. Others would not be harmed in any way. However, using this method is both expensive and time-consuming.

Seeking a Solution

The demand of sheepmen that they be allowed by law to use poisoned bait and steel traps is raising questions in the minds of many. Environmentalists who want to protect wildlife say that sheep-owners not only get money from the government when their profits are low, but also pay far too little for the right to graze their flocks on public lands. In addition, a vast amount of land that belongs to the public, and on which all of us pay taxes, is being ruined by overgrazing.

Many environmentalists also question just how sheep-raisers got along for thousands of years before they could use government land, often without payment, and depend on the government to help them through bad years. A few go to the extreme and urge that sheepmen in trouble should just get out of the business. This, to put it bluntly, seems stupid.

We *need* sheep. Unlike cattle, they furnish us with two valuable products. Sheep can change rough pasture grass into good protein, suitable for human beings to eat, much better than cattle can, and they make use of plants that cattle would not touch. In this time of world food shortages we need to keep and use all available means of providing wholesome food.

Also, wool is a natural fiber, and can be produced as long as sheep are grown. Synthetic fibers, on the other hand, are made from chemicals obtained from fossil fuel. With oil growing ever more scarce and expensive, synthetic materials may someday cost far more than wool.

Although sheep-raising should be encouraged, and helped when necessary, this ought not to be done by ruining public land—or private land. Furthermore, both predators and prey of whatever kind should be kept under control, but there is no good reason why any species should be completely wiped out. Each kind is needed if we are to keep a proper balance in nature.

We have interfered with this process by choosing a few plants and animals that we want to produce in vast numbers for our own use. This upsets the balance, and it is up to us to find a way to set up a new system that will work. We have had little experience in this sort of thing, and we make many mistakes, but we have learned one fact: getting rid of predators completely does not mean that other animals will therefore be healthy and thriving.

Today biologists in many states are hard at work looking for practical and useful methods of control that will help sheepmen. Finding an answer that will help save the animals and at the same time not destroy wildlife needlessly will take brains and training, as well as money for research. Colleges and universities, and the scientists themselves, are trying to furnish the brains and training. Perhaps if sheepmen, environmentalists, and politicians will give them enough time, and help out with some of the money needed for research, they may be able to find a solution that all can accept.

Relationships of the Goat-Sheep Subfamily

Order: Artiodactyls—Even-toed ungulates (hoofed mammals) including pigs, camels, and ruminants

Suborder: Ruminants—Cud-chewers, including animals with antlers and those with horns

Family: Horned ungulates—Hollow-horned, even-toed hoofed mammals, including cattle, antelopes, goats, and sheep

Subfamily: Caprines—Goat-sheep tribe and their relatives

Tribe: Goat-sheep

True goats (caprids): wild goat, ibex, markhor, domestic goat

True sheep: mouflon, urial, argali, snow sheep, Dall sheep, bighorns, domestic sheep

Part goat, part sheep: tahr, aoudad (Barbary sheep), bharal (blue sheep)

Tribe: Rock goats—chamois, mountain goat }
Tribe: Goral—goral, serow   } GOAT-ANTELOPES

Tribe: Takin   }
Tribe: Musk ox } OX-GOATS

Suggested Reading

Books

Bronson, Wilfred S., *Goats* (Harcourt Brace, N.Y., 1959)

Burton, Maurice, and Robert Burton, Eds., *International Wildlife Encyclopedia* (20 vols.; Marshall Cavendish, New York, 1970)

Carrington, Richard, and Eds. of Time-Life Books, *The Mammals* (Time-Life Books, N.Y., 1975)

Cavanna, Betty, and George Russell Harrison, *The First Book of Wool* (Franklin Watts, New York, 1966)

Clark, Joseph D., *Beastly Folklore* (Scarecrow Press, Metuchen, N.J., 1968)

Cohan, Roy, *How to Make It on the Land* (Prentice Hall, Englewood Cliffs, N.J., 1972)

Crandall, Lee S., *Management of Wild Animals in Captivity* (University of Chicago Press, Chicago, 1964)

Dixon, Paige, *Summer of the White Goat* (Atheneum, N.Y., 1977; well researched fiction about a young man observing mountain goats)

Geist, Valerius, *Mountain Sheep: A Study in Behavior and Evolution* (University of Chicago Press, Chicago, 1971)

Gersh, Harry, *The Animals Next Door: A Guide to Zoos and Aquariums of the Americas* (Fleet Academic Editions, N.Y., 1971)

Grzimek, Bernhard, *Animal Life Encyclopedia*, vols. 12, 13 (Van Nostrand Reinhold, New York, 1972)

Hamblin, Dora Jean, and Eds. of Time-Life Books, *The First Cities* (Time-Life Books, N.Y., 1973)

Hyams, Edward, *Animals in the Service of Man* (Lippincott, Phila., 1972)

Leonard, Jonathan N., and Eds. of Time-Life Books, *The First Farmers* (Time-Life Books, N.Y., 1973)

Morris, Desmond, *The Mammals: A Guide to the Living Species* (Harper and Row, N.Y., 1965)

Readings from *Scientific American: Early Man in America* (Freeman, San Francisco, 1971)

Roots, Clive, *Animal Invaders* (Universe Books, New York, 1976)

Sanderson, Ivan T., *Living Mammals of the World* (Doubleday, Garden City, N.Y., 1972)

Schultz, Gwen, *Ice Age Lost* (Doubleday, Garden City, N.Y., 1974)

Wendt, Herbert, *Before the Deluge*, trans. from the German by Richard and Clara Winston (Doubleday, Garden City, N.Y., 1968)

Magazines

Audubon, "Bighorn Profile" (Nov. 1973)

Brooks, James W., "Wildlife in Alaska" (*National Parks and Conservation Magazine*, Nov. 1970)

Bruemmer, Fred, "Ill Shapen Beast" (*Natural History*, March 1968; musk ox)

————, "Saga of the Ox" (*International Wildlife*, July-Aug. 1976)

Carmichel, Jim, "Hunt for Chamois and Tahr" (*Outdoor Life*, July 1975)

Coblentz, Bruce E., "Wild Goats of Santa Catalina" (*Natural History*, June-July, 1976)

Cooperative Farmer, "Small, But Mighty Milkmakers" (April, 1976)

Dalrymple, Byron W., "Bighorns of the Big Bend" (*Outdoor Life*, June 1973)

Frome, Michael, "Crusade for Wildlife: Grazing Sheep Destroy the Lands That Belong to All Americans" (*Defenders of Wildlife*, April 1976)

George, Jean Craighead, "Secrets of the Elusive Mountain Goat" (*National Wildlife*, Dec.-Jan. 1977)

Hughes, J. Donald, "The Ancient Roots of Our Ecological Crisis" (*National Parks and Conservation Magazine*, Oct. 1975)

Kraft, Virginia, "Wild Sheep in a Woolly Land" (*Sports Illustrated,* June 26, 1972)

Laycock, George, "Dilemma in the Desert: Bighorns or Burros?" (*Audubon,* Sept. 1974)

———, "Our Adopted Wildlife" (*National Wildlife,* Feb.-Mar. 1966)

Life, "Return of the Musk Ox" (Sept. 15, 1967)

———, "Showdown on the Salmon River Range" (May 22, 1970)

———, "Tell Me That U Mishmi, Gracie" (Nov. 5, 1971)

———, "Wait Till Next Year" (July 15, 1966; takin)

Morgan, James K., "Last Stand for the Bighorn" (*National Geographic,* Sept. 1973)

———, "Slamming the Ram into Oblivion" (*Audubon,* Nov. 1973)

Murphy, Robert, "This Animal Walks Up Walls" (*National Wildlife,* Apr.-May 1971)

National Parks and Conservation Magazine, "Goats in the Parks" (Nov. 1971)

———, "New Mexico's Four-Footed Refugees" (Nov. 1965)

National Wildlife, "The Renegades" (Aug.-Sept. 1966; feral animals)

Newsweek, "Ghoulies, Ghosties . . ." (July 13, 1959; takin)

———, "The Bighorn's Last Stand" (Mar. 15, 1971)

Nicholds, Elizabeth, "The Goats of Thunder Hill" (*National Geographic,* May 1954)

Noblecourt, Christiane Desroches, "Tutankhamun's Golden Trove" (*National Geographic,* Oct. 1963)

O'Connor, Jack, "The Stories Sheep Horns Tell" (*Outdoor Life,* Feb. 1974)

Page, Warren, "The Sheep That Is a Goat" (*Field and Stream,* June 1971)

Pappenheimer, John R., "The Sleep Factor" (*Scientific American,* Aug. 1976)

Pringle, Laurence, "Each Antagonist in Coyote Debate Is Partly Correct" (*Smithsonian,* Mar. 1975)

Randall, Dick, "The Poison Scene" (*Defenders of Wildlife,* Apr. 1976)

Reiger, George, "In the War on Predators There Is No Middle Ground" (*National Wildlife,* June-July 1974)

Ricciuti, Edward R., "Spirit of the Summits" (*International Wildlife*, Nov.-Dec. 1976)

Rideout, Chester B., "Goats of Gunsight Pass" (*National Parks and Conservation Magazine*, Feb. 1974)

Saturday Review, "Domesticating the Musk Ox: The Gentle Agriculture" (June 10, 1972)

Schaller, George B., "Stalking the Wild Sheep of Kalabagh" (*International Wildlife*, July 1975)

———, "The Sheep That Isn't" (*Animal Kingdom*, Feb.-Mar. 1977)

Science News Letter, "Big Game For U.S." (July 4, 1959)

Scientific American, "Self-Shearing Sheep" (Dec. 1968)

Scott, Jack Denton, "His Friends Call Him Billy" (*National Wildlife*, Apr.-May 1972)

———, "Musk Ox, It Fed the Cave Man" (*International Wildlife*, Sept.-Oct. 1972)

———, "No One Really Knows the Chamois" (*International Wildlife*, Sept.-Oct. 1971)

Sokolov, Raymond, "The Gifts of the Goat" (*Natural History*, Oct. 1975)

Sports Illustrated, "New Game in New Mexico" (May 27, 1963)

———, "The Golden Shmoo of the Barren Land" (July 17, 1967; musk ox)

Teal, John J., Jr., "Domesticating the Wild and Woolly Musk Ox" (*National Geographic*, June 1970)

Tennesen, Michael, "Bighorn on the Run" (*National Wildlife*, Oct.-Nov. 1975)

Time, "How to Peel a Sheep" (Dec. 13, 1968)

Valdez, Raul, and Leticia Alamia, "Fecund Mouflon" (*Natural History*, Nov. 1977)

Zeldin, Marvin, "Update: Coyotes and Lambs" (*Audubon*, Mar. 1975)

Index

105747

DATE DUE

DEC 2 0 1983			
NOV 1 3 1989			
NOV 2 6 1991			
AUG 17 2003			

J
599.735
J
Jenkins, Marie M.
Goats, sheep, and how they live.

Ohio Dominican College Library
1216 Sunbury Road
Columbus, Ohio 43219

DEMCO